UNDERSTANDING

THE FOAL

YOUR **GUIDE** TO HORSE HEALTH
CARE AND MANAGEMENT

Copyright © 1998, 2002 The Blood-Horse, Inc.
All Rights reserved. No part of this book may be repro-
duced in any form by any means, including photocopying,
audio recording, or any information storage or retrieval system, without the permission in writing from the copyright
holder. Inquiries should be addressed to Publisher, The
Blood-Horse, Inc., Box 4038, Lexington, KY 40544-4038.

ISBN 1-58150-006-8

Printed in the United States of America
First Edition: December 1998
2 3 4 5 6 7 8 9 10

UNDERSTANDING
THE FOAL

YOUR **GUIDE** TO HORSE HEALTH CARE AND MANAGEMENT

By Christina S. Cable, DVM
Foreword by A. C. Asbury, DVM, Diplomate ACT

The Blood-Horse, Inc. Lexington, KY

Other titles offered by
The Horse Health Care Library

Understanding EPM

Understanding Equine Lameness

Understanding Equine First Aid

Understanding The Equine Foot

Understanding Equine Nutrition

Understanding Laminitis

Contents

FOREWORD

The normal and abnormal events involved in late-term pregnancy, in delivery of the foal, and its early development must be understood to some degree if horse breeders are to be successful. In *Understanding the Foal*, Dr. Christina Cable takes us through these processes in a clear and well-organized discussion, explaining the important steps along the way and pointing out the critical management and health considerations necessary to raise a healthy foal.

For the novice and non-professional breeder, this volume should be required reading. The key ingredients for those readers are consistent references to spotting trouble early. In the sphere of foaling mares and rearing foals, recognition of problems before they develop fully is a must. Dr. Cable's management experiences and medical expertise provide the breeder with guidelines that can mean the difference in every potential pitfall on the road to productive foal rearing.

While the professional and long-term breeder or farm manager might find some of the discussions elementary, there are many good reasons for them to investigate this book as well. After all, experts often proceed through the steps of management that have been time-tested without fully understanding the underlying processes. Also, some differences of opinion on the traditional methods are often good seeds for further consideration of your methods.

Understanding the Foal takes you through the late stages of pregnancy, provides a clear picture of the stages of labor, and guides you through the perils of the early days of a foal's life. Among the most useful sections are those dealing with passive transfer of antibodies from the mare to the foal and the potential neonatal diseases and disorders. Basic mare and foal management processes that are well covered include feeding, handling, and routine applications of preventive medicine.

A. C. Asbury, DVM, Diplomate ACT
Professor Emeritus
Department of Large Animal Clinical Sciences
University of Florida

INTRODUCTION

People raise foals for many reasons. Monetary considerations are a factor for commercial breeders, for instance, while the sheer thrill of producing a foal from a beloved pleasure horse or champion competitor motivates others. Whatever the reason, foals entail a lot of responsibility. Although the arrival of a foal signifies the culmination of 11 months of planning, waiting, and dreaming, once that foal takes its first breath the owner or caretaker must temper sentiment with good management.

Understanding the Foal was written out of my love for foals and the wonderful mares that deliver them into this world. From the first time I witnessed a foaling, until now — 15 years later — the magic has never ended. Despite the magic, I firmly believe that raising healthy foals is not a result of good luck, but the result of good management. Experience also counts for quite a bit, as recognizing a problem early can help reduce death and disease in foals. This book is meant as a guide for owners, farm managers, and anyone who is raising a single foal or 100 foals on a large breeding farm. *Understanding the Foal* is by no means intended as a substitute for regular veterinary care, but to help educate the reader about techniques on how to prepare for the birth of a foal and how to raise a foal in a healthy environment.

This book also encourages the reader to increase his or her powers of observation to help recognize problems in a timely fashion. Knowing what to look for often is the key. I cannot overemphasize the importance of early recognition in preventing or dealing successfully with problems the foal or mare might develop. I also want to stress that you should never be afraid to ask your veterinarian to evaluate your mare or foal if you suspect a problem as you know them best.

Understanding the Foal is organized in a step-by-step fashion and discusses late-term mares, the birth process, caring and monitoring neonates, and caring for weanlings. If you want to read further on the topic of foals, a recommended reading list is at the end of this book.

Christina S. Cable, DVM
Cornell University
Ithaca, New York

CHAPTER 1

The Late-Term Mare

Ever since I can remember, I have been entranced with mares and their foals. I have spent a lifetime learning how to care for them and how best to raise healthy foals. As a veterinarian, the best skill I have developed is the power of observation. I cannot stress enough the importance of developing this skill when you raise horses. Although horses cannot talk directly with humans, their language is easy to understand once you know how to observe them. Throughout this book, I will emphasize the need to monitor your mare and its foal closely so you can learn what is normal for both animals and thus recognize abnormalities which might signify medical problems.

Although this book is entitled *Understanding the Foal*, you must start with a healthy mare in order to have a healthy foal. For more information on the subject of broodmare health, please refer to another book in this series, *Understanding the Broodmare*. In this book, I pick up the story and discuss the late-term mare, a mare in the last month of gestation.

BROODMARE CARE — HEALTH RECORDS

The first step in caring for your mare is to keep very good health records. These records can be invaluable and should include vaccinations, breeding dates, prior gestational lengths, illnesses, and medical treatment. The health records on the mare's previous foals are also important. Breeding dates help determine when a mare is due to foal and gives

you time to make the necessary prepara- tions. Mares often repeat their gestation- al length, so any marked variation war- rants an investigation. Furthermore, if the mare were to become ill during the last months of pregnancy,

Keep good records.

knowing her previous gestation period(s) might help the vet- erinarian and owner decide on a course of treatment, such as inducing labor, performing a Caesarean section if the foal is fully developed, or terminating the pregnancy by aborting the fetus. Knowing the breeding dates will help you make an informed, prompt decision on whether the foal will be able to handle life outside of the womb. When the vet arrives on an emergency call, having this information at your fingertips can save a great deal of time, anxiety, and possibly the life of the mare and foal.

The health record can be as simple as filling out all of the necessary information on a sheet of paper kept in a spiral notebook or composition book. Or you may choose to fill in a form supplied by your veterinarian. Any way you do it, the information can be life saving.

VACCINATIONS

The foal is an almost defenseless creature, born without any antibodies capable of fighting off infection. The equine pla- centa does not allow crossover of antibodies from the mare to the foal in utero. The mare makes up for this quirk of nature by producing large quantities of antibodies in the "first milk" or colostrum. After it is born, her foal will get all of the antibodies it needs to fight off infection during the critical first few weeks of life by drinking the mare's colostrum. We will discuss the problems associated with failure of the foal to consume colostrum in a later chapter. Because of the impor-

Keep mare inoculations up to date.

tance of good-quality colostrum, it is imperative to vaccinate the mare a month to six weeks before she gives birth so that her colostrum contains as many antibodies as possible. Routine vaccinations at this time include tetanus toxoid, influenza, Eastern and Western en-

cephalitis, and rabies. Other vaccinations which might need to be administered include the *Clostridium botulinum* toxoid, and the vaccine for rhino-pneumonitis (equine herpes virus I & IV). The rhino-pneumonitis vaccinations might be recommended throughout pregnancy at gestational months five, seven, and nine to protect the mare from health problems that increase the risk of abortion. Please discuss with your veterinarian whether or not your mare requires these vaccinations if she is at risk of exposure to this virus.

FEEDING

The late-term mare uses a great deal of energy to support the foal that is growing rapidly within her uterus. Failure to feed the mare enough food to generate this energy will usually result in a normal-sized foal, but at the expense of the mare's condition. A study by Auburn University researchers Pugh and Schumaker on feeding pregnant mares found that in their last trimester they required a 20% increase in energy requirements and a 32% increase in protein requirements —

an amount well above the normal maintenance levels of feed needed by mature horses. The late-term mare usually needs to consume more energy than what she can derive from eating grass alone.

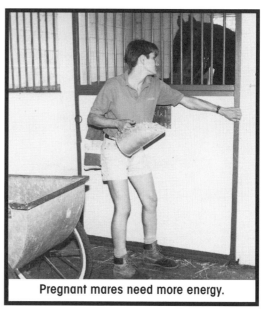

Pregnant mares need more energy.

Furthermore, for many breeds it is desirable to have foals born early in the year and the mares will foal when there is still snow on the ground. For this reason, mares should be allowed to eat free choice grass or grass/alfalfa mix hay, especially during their last trimester of pregnancy. They also should receive a high-quality feed or pelleted ration. The amount should be tailored to the individual to prevent obesity or severe weight loss. One of the findings in the study by Pugh and Schumaker recommended feeding a late-term mare between one-quarter and three-quarters of a pound of grain per 100 pounds of body weight per day. Pregnant mares always should have free access to clean water.

SUPPLEMENTS

Depending on where you live, your mare also might need supplements to get the necessary vitamins and trace minerals. All mares should have access to a trace mineral block during pregnancy. Some areas of the country are very low in selenium and vitamin E. Supplementation is crucial in preventing white muscle disease in the foal and could help prevent the mare from retaining the placenta. Many areas of the country also contain other natural hazards. In areas that have fescue grass pastures, mares can ingest a fungus (*Acremonium coenophialum*) that likes to grow on fescue. If the fungus is ingested in the last trimester of pregnancy, it can lead to agalactia (lack of milk production), prolonged gestation and resulting dystocia (difficult birth), thickened placentas, and/or abortion. If you have mares grazing fescue pastures, they need to be removed from the pasture during the last three to four months of gestation and fed good-quality hay (not fescue) in order to prevent these complications.

THE CASLICK'S

Besides vaccinations, one of the early preparations for foaling is removing the Caslick's. A Caslick's procedure is commonly performed on broodmares. It involves suturing

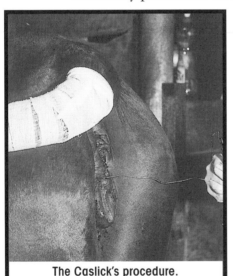

The Caslick's procedure.

the upper part of the vulvar lips together to prevent contamination of feces into the vaginal cavity during pregnancy. If this was performed on your mare soon after she was bred, then you need to have the sutured part opened by your veterinarian. This involves anesthetizing the area of the Caslick's with a local anesthetic such as lidocaine, which is similar to the Novocain your dentist uses for oral surgery. After the vulva is desensitized, then the veterinarian uses a scalpel blade to open the vulva lips. Failure to have the Caslick's removed can result in a dystocia and/or the tearing of the vulva during the birthing process, plus the possibility of a perineal body laceration.

The Caslick's can be removed at one to two weeks prior to foaling. At this time, your veterinarian can evaluate the mare for readiness to give birth and ensure that there are no obvious signs of abnormalities with the mare and foal.

SUPPLIES FOR FOALING

Several weeks before the expected due date, you should begin to prepare for the foal's delivery. Some mares can surprise you with an early delivery, and you don't want to be caught off guard. First, you should discuss whether you want your veterinarian to be present for the delivery. If your veterinarian is going to be present, then obtain all the phone numbers, beeper numbers, and cellular phone numbers to contact the vet when the time comes. If your mare has had problems in the past or is a high-risk mare, then having your veterinarian present would be a good idea. Just in case you need to take the mare and newborn foal to an emergency clinic, have your truck and trailer ready to use at a moment's notice.

Regardless of whether or not your veterinarian will be attending the birth, there are a few supplies you should have ready for the delivery.

These include:

• a halter and lead shank for the mare

• blankets and/or clean towels to dry the foal

• disinfectant such as Betadine or chlorhexidine to be diluted with sterile saline for umbilical dips

• umbilical tape in order to tie off the umbilical stump in case of hemorrhage

• scissors

• a bucket in which to place the placenta or after birth for further examination by the veterinarian

• rectal sleeves and sterile lubricant

• a watch for timing the different stages of labor

• a rectal thermometer

• a stethoscope (to monitor the mare or foal's heart rate and respiratory rate)

• Fleet enemas or enema tubing (supplied by your veterinarian) plus a gentle soap such as Ivory

These supplies can be placed in the barn's medical kit or kept in a tack trunk so the supplies will be on hand and ready to use at any time. Many of these supplies, such as the umbilical tape, can be used for problems before your veterinarian arrives. Before the birth of your foal, you should become familiar with how to take a temperature on a horse as well as the heart rate and respiratory rate using your stethoscope. Ask your veterinarian to show you how to perform these tasks. The information you gain by performing these simple procedures can give your veterinarian invaluable information about the condition of your mare and its foal.

FOALING AREAS

I cannot stress enough the importance of allowing the mare to foal in a large, clean, and dry area. I cannot express how frustrating it is to treat a foal for septicemia (infection throughout the body) when I see that the foal has been living in a manure-laden stall or paddock. Where foals are concerned, cleanliness is next to Godliness.

A foaling stall should be roomy.

A foaling stall should be at least 14 x 14 feet in size. Some mares are allowed to foal in paddocks on the grass. This is perfectly acceptable if the location is clean, dry, and has protection against the weather, such as a shed or large trees. Foaling stalls make it easier for someone to observe the mare at regular intervals and during the night. Stalls also offer warmth and protection against occasional predators such as packs of roaming dogs. Before placing a mare in a foaling stall, disinfect it. The foaling stall should be well-bedded, well-ventilated, and clean. Remember, foals are very susceptible to infection. Clean the stall of all manure and wet bedding at least twice a day and preferably multiple times a day. It is not acceptable for a newborn to be delivered into this world directly into a pile of horse manure.

INDIVIDUAL MARE BREEDING RECORD

Mare:_____ Clinic number _____

Age: _____ Breed: _____

Owner:_____ Phone: _____

Mare to be bred by _____ fresh _____ fresh-shipped _____ frozen semen?

Date of arrival: _____ Date of departure: _____

Mare's status: maiden _____   maiden prev. bred _____

                   open _____   barren _____

Aborted: single _____ twins _____ days _____

Foaling mare: date of last OV: _____ due date:_____

_____

Stallion: _____

Stallion Owner:_____

Phone: _____

Other info: _____

CHAPTER 2

Preparing for Foaling

The normal gestation period for mares can range from 320 to 350 days. However, normal, healthy foals have been delivered anywhere from 305 to 360 days from their date of conception. Foals born before day 300 are considered nonviable; they will rarely live. Foals born between day 300 and 320 are often weak and have low birth weights. Although such foals are usually considered premature, they have a reasonable chance of survival with intensive care. Some mares carry their foals for a "normal" gestational length, then deliver an apparently premature foal called a "dysmature" foal. Development of such foals has not been completed by their apparently normal gestational length. These foals often show the physical characteristics of premature foals — silky coats, pliant ears, and low birth weights. Some mares, on the other hand, might

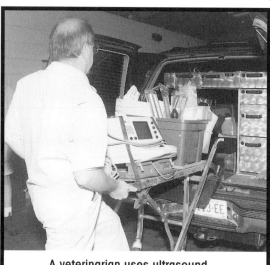

A veterinarian uses ultrasound...

have an extended pregnancy and deliver normal-size, healthy foals.

Eleven months is a very long time to anticipate the birth of a foal. A great deal of hope, excitement, and dreams can accompany the time an owner spends waiting for the birth of a foal. Breeding horses is both a financial investment and a very rewarding process. Since the largest part of the investment usually comes well before the birth date, losing a foal because its birth is unattended is a

AT A GLANCE

• Normal gestation ranges from 320 to 350 days, but can be shorter or longer.

• Most mares foal without complications.

• Electrolyte levels can help predict when a mare will foal.

• Closed circuit televisions and foal alert devices can be useful in monitoring pregnant mares.

tragedy. Therefore, most cost-conscious and sensible owners want to monitor the birth of the foal to make sure nothing goes wrong. About 90% of the time, the birth goes as nature intended, but there are times when human intervention is necessary. Being right there when an emergency arises can

make the difference between a healthy newborn foal and one that does not survive.

Most mares like to foal when it is quiet. They prefer to be undisturbed. They have a natural instinct to wait for such conditions in order to protect their foals from predators.

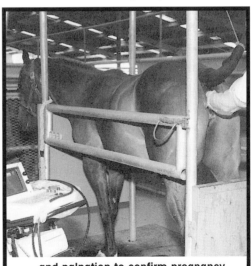

...and palpation to confirm pregnancy.

Therefore, your mare probably will not deliver her foal at your convenience. Most mares foal either late at night or in the wee hours of the morning. Consequently, close monitoring of the late-term mare for sometimes weeks at a time is the only way to ensure that the birth is attended. Close monitoring can come in the form of a closed circuit television, hiring a nightwatch person, or sending the mare to a special care facility for foaling. Otherwise, you might have many sleepless nights.

MONITORING THE LATE-TERM MARE

A late-term mare (one within the last month of gestation), should be evaluated at least once a day for physical changes

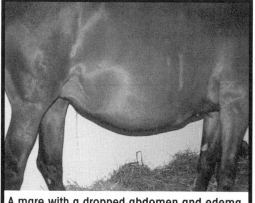

A mare with a dropped abdomen and edema. She foaled two days later.

that will indicate her readiness to give birth. The late-term mare will develop an enlarged abdomen which begins to drop as she nears foaling. The other physical changes that indicate readiness to give birth are swelling and vulvar laxity (the elongation of the vulvar lips), the relaxation of the pelvic ligaments (sinking of the muscles on either side of the tailhead), and udder enlargement, possibly accompanied by milky secretions.

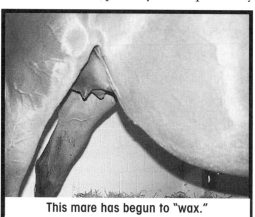

This mare has begun to "wax."

The mare's mammary glands will begin to enlarge in the last month of her pregnancy. Close to the time she foals, these secretions will change from a watery, clear, or straw colored fluid to a thick, white, milky fluid. As the mare gets very close to delivering, she will produce colostrum (first milk), which is thick, yellow, and very sticky. "Waxing" is when the colostrum drips from the mare's teats. Once a mare begins "waxing," then the birth is very close. However, mares which have already delivered several foals might drip milk for days to weeks before foaling, so this sign does not always mean that birth is imminent. That is one of the reasons closely monitoring the late-term mare is so important.

Mares can undergo any number of behavioral changes in addition to the physical changes during the early stages of labor. They show these behavior changes during the first stage of labor, including pawing, getting up and down frequently, curling the upper lip (flehmen), yawning, restlessness, sweating, stretching to urinate and/or defecating small amounts frequently, and looking at their flanks.

Many mares need privacy when labor begins. Loud noises or distractions from people or horses can cause the mare to delay labor. Keep the barn quiet and do not disturb the mare by crowding her stall if you think labor will begin soon.

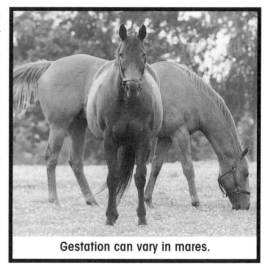
Gestation can vary in mares.

PREDICTING FOALING

Several years ago, predicting the foaling time was based solely on the physical signs of impending birth discussed earlier. Only close monitoring of the mare could ensure an attended foaling. Even though close monitoring of late-term mares remains important, predicting foaling is studied not only to predict when a mare is going to foal naturally, but to determine when the mare is ready to foal. Or, to put it more accurately, to predict when the foal is ready to adapt to life outside of the uterus. Remember, the mare begins to show external signs of impending birth as the foal develops and matures inside the uterus.

Unlike humans, the length of pregnancy in mares is not related solely to fetal maturation. In humans, it can be safe to induce labor if a woman is in the last two weeks or so of a pregnancy. The baby will be mature. In horses, the length of pregnancy varies so greatly that you cannot rely on counting days on a calendar to determine if the foal is mature. This is extremely important for mares which need to have the birth process induced (begun artificially) so that they can be attended. For example, mares with pre-pubic tendon ruptures (the tearing of the ligament that supports the abdomen) might need to have labor induced. Loss of this structure makes it impossible for a mare to contract her abdominal muscles and deliver the foal normally. The attending veterinarian needs to know when the foal is ready to be born. If the mare's labor is induced when the foal is not ready to handle life outside the uterus, the foal might need serious intensive care to survive. If very premature, the foal could die despite intensive care.

Searching for a more accurate gauge of a mare's readiness to foal, researchers have been studying electrolytes (the minerals calcium, potassium, and sodium produced in the pre-foaling milk). Electrolyte changes and concentrations within the milk have been shown to be associated with the foal's level of maturity. As a result of such studies, several methods are now used to predict when a mare is going to foal. Calcium is the most often monitored electrolyte in mare's milk. It is logical to think that the calcium concentration will increase as the mare draws closer to foaling.

In one study, researchers found that when calcium concentrations in the pre-foaling milk are low, there is only a small chance for a mare to foal within the next 24 hours.

However, when calcium concentrations are greater than 200 parts per million (ppm), then there is a 51% chance that the mare will foal in 24 hours, an 84% chance that she will foal in 48 hours, and a 97% chance that she will foal in 72 hours. This is the basis for the product called the FoalWatch Kit. The kit is used to test the mare's milk once a day, usually in the morning. First, her milk is diluted with distilled water. Then an indicator dye is added to show the amount of calcium carbonate in ppm in the diluted sample. When the ppm of calcium carbonate reach 200, it indicates the mare's readiness to give birth.

There are several types of test kits to measure the calcium or calcium and magnesium of the mare's milk. Calcium also can be measured by automated chemistry tests. The level of calcium in the milk which indicates readiness to give birth has been shown to be greater than 40 milligrams per deciliter. As with any test, 100% accuracy is not always possible. Some mares will produce maximum calcium concentration before the day of parturition (birth). These tests can help determine when not to attend a mare at night.

Other kits available include the Predict-a-Foal test kit which measures calcium and magnesium levels in the milk. This test provides a strip with five indicators which correlate to different levels of calcium and magnesium in the milk. If only one or none of the squares changes color, then the mare has a 1% chance of foaling in the next 12 hours. When four to five of the squares change color, there is an 80% chance of foaling within the next 12 hours.

OTHER ELECTROLYTES

Another method for detecting readiness to give birth is to measure the electrolytes sodium and potassium in pre-foaling milk. During the last week of pregnancy, the mare's milk will undergo marked changes in these electrolytes along with the increase in calcium concentration. The sodium levels will decrease as the potassium levels increase (inversion). These electrolytes can be charted on a graph to follow their respective increases or decreases. Eventually, the two lines intersect, and when the potassium levels become greater than the sodium levels in the milk, it is a strong indicator of readiness for birth. The potassium concentration in pre-foaling milk is usually higher than the sodium concentration within 24 hours of parturition.

Electrolyte levels can serve as useful indicators in a mare's readiness to give birth. Veterinarians can use calcium, sodium, and potassium values along with the physical examination findings to determine very accurately when a foal will be mature enough to induce labor in a mare. Milk should be evaluated daily from 10 days before the due date or whenever she begins to produce milk. This will help determine more accurately when the foal is ready to be delivered.

CLOSED CIRCUIT TELEVISION

Watching a closed circuit television is a very convenient way to monitor the mare, because you do not have to travel out to the barn to check on her. You can watch the mare from your house or from a separate room in the barn so that she will remain undisturbed. The disadvantage of this monitoring system is that the mare might place herself in a position not easily seen by the television camera. Most importantly, someone still has to monitor her by watching the television screen throughout the night, otherwise you might not notice her until she has gone into labor. Many breeding farms and veterinary clinics use a closed circuit television to monitor late-term mares.

LABOR ALERT DEVICES

Another method of monitoring the mare is a labor alert device. The Foalert system is composed of a transmitter which is attached to the vulva of the mare. When the vulvar lips separate, the transmitter sends a signal to the receiver. It sounds an alarm to alert the person doing the monitoring.

This is a good system, but the person must remain close to the mare at all times, because the device only alerts you when the mare has gone into labor. If you arrive just 30 minutes after the alarm sounds, you might be too late.

A similar system is the Breeder Protech 2000, which operates on the same principle as the Foalert system. A transmitter is encased in a sponge, which is placed in the mare's vagina. When the mare is in labor, the sponge and transmitter are expelled from the vagina. Then the change in ambient temperature activates the transmitter. Again, it notifies the attendant that there is a labor in progress. You should discuss these options with your veterinarian and decide which is right for you and your mare.

CHAPTER 3

Understanding Labor

Once labor begins for your mare, the 11 months you have spent waiting, expecting, planning, and hoping are over. All will be realized or lost in a few hours. Time is of the essence because a horse's labor can be a very explosive, fast-moving, 30-minute event. If you understand what is happening, it will help you recognize a potential problem and get help. This chapter will cover a description of normal labor and what you should expect to see. It will also cover potential birthing problems.

STAGE I LABOR

Labor in the mare is classified in three stages. Stage I is the period when the uterus begins to contract. The contractions vary in intensity, and can be suspended by the mare if conditions are unfavorable for foaling. The principal functions of stage I are to begin putting pressure on the cervix to start dilation and to initiate the movements of the fetus by which it will eventually position itself for birth.

An interesting study of pony mares 20 years ago by Drs. Jeffcott and Rossdale used X-rays to monitor the movements of the fetus during the various stages of labor. This proved conclusively that the foal is an active participant in the process of positioning. During the latter half of gestation the foal is on its back, with the legs folded somewhat and the head down between the forelegs. When labor commences and the uterus begins to tighten, the foal reaches back with the forelegs and head, toward the pelvic canal. As labor progresses into the second stage, this positioning enables the foal to rotate so that its head and forefeet are right side up as they enter the canal (the "diver's" position). At this time, the rear quarters are still "sitting" on the floor of the uterus. The final rotation that brings the foal into the proper alignment is in the last expulsion through the birth canal. This phenomenon is mentioned for more than just its unique nature. It is now evident that failure of positioning is frequently due to an abnormal or weak foal which cannot position himself for those early steps. Many foalings which are difficult due to the legs or

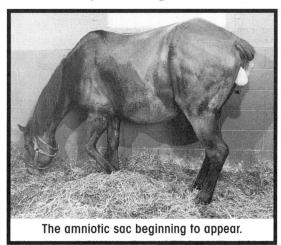

The amniotic sac beginning to appear.

head being turned back can be explained by disease or development problems that render the foal unable to participate.

In stage I the mare acts restless, frequently getting up and down, urinating often, pawing, and sweating (acting colicky). This stage of labor can last anywhere from 20 minutes to several hours. The mare should not be disturbed during this time because she might delay her delivery of the foal if she feels nervous or uncomfortable. If you plan to have your vet present for the delivery, call now.

As the mare's labor progresses, her contractions will push the foal and the surrounding membrane (chorioallantoic membrane) into the cervix. Eventually the membrane will break, releasing her "water" (amber-colored allantoic fluid).

Before her water breaks, if the mare seems comfortable with someone in the stall with her, wrap her tail and clean her vulva with warm water and soap (liquid soap or Betadine).

STAGE II LABOR

Active contractions will begin within a few minutes of the mare's water breaking and the mare will begin pushing actively. During this stage of labor, the foal will be delivered.

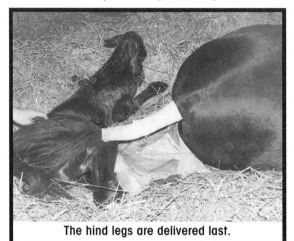

The mare's contractions are very forceful and the foal must be delivered within 30 to 40 minutes or is in danger of suffocating. The mare might get up once or twice during this stage of labor, but most often lies on her side to push (lateral recumbency). The amniotic

The hind legs are delivered last.

sac will protrude first from the vulva as the contractions begin. The foal should present with its front feet, soles pointing down, covered with the amniotic sac, which is milky white. The front legs usually are presented one before the other. As the contractions continue, the foal's head emerges, with its chin resting on the two front legs. After the front legs and head are visible, the mare will really begin to push hard. One of the foal's shoulders followed by the other will be expelled, then the torso. Next the foal's hips and hind legs slide out of the birth canal.

At this point, the foal should be on the ground, although one foot still might be inside the mare. The mare should be resting quietly. The amnion usually ruptures when shoulders are delivered. If the amnion around the foal has not ruptured during the delivery, you should open the sac gently and remove the membranes from around the foal's nose and muzzle. Within a few minutes of birth, the foal should be breathing comfortably, struggling to raise its head, and getting into a position of sternal recumbency. If the mare and foal are both resting comfortably and quietly, they should be left undisturbed. During this quiet time, leaving the umbilical cord attached will allow a substantial amount of blood to be transferred from the placenta to the foal. The mare will break the cord when she stands.

STAGE III LABOR

During this stage, the mare should expel the placenta and her uterus will begin to return to normal size (involute). In the time it takes to complete this process, you should pick up the dangling placenta before it hits the floor of the stall. The placenta should be tied to itself with umbilical tape or twine to keep it from being stepped on or becoming entangled in the mare's hind legs. Once the placenta has been passed, remove it from the stall or paddock and place in a bucket for your veterinarian to examine later. The veterinarian should examine the placenta to determine if all of it has been passed and if there is any evidence of placentitis (infection within the placenta), which could put your foal at risk of becoming sick. The placenta usually is passed within 30 minutes of parturition and should not take more than three hours.

As the uterus is involuting, the mare might show signs of mild colic, such as pawing, straining to urinate, or urinating frequently. However, her discomfort should pass relatively quickly (within 30 minutes). If it lasts for more than one hour or she becomes more uncomfortable, have your veterinarian examine her immediately.

Now that I have described how a normal labor should progress, I will review the different stages and talk about some of the more common problems that might arise. By the time your mare goes into labor, you'll want to know what to look out for and when to call for help.

PROLONGED STAGE I LABOR OR COLIC

What happens when things do not go as you expect them to? Your late-term mare seems to be going into stage I labor, although she hasn't really shown any other signs of impending parturition (lack of udder development, no relaxation of vulva). She remains uncomfortable for several hours, rolling and pawing. What should you do? Have the mare examined by your veterinarian. Abdominal pain, or colic, is an emergency at any time, but it can be especially troublesome when the mare is carrying a foal. Most of the time, the colic is just an ordinary case of indigestion. However, the colic could be more serious and should be evaluated by a veterinarian.

Late-term mares also can develop a uterine torsion (twisting of the uterus), which requires correction. Sometimes the torsion can be corrected without surgery by anesthetizing the mare, then rolling her over. If that doesn't work, the alternative is surgery.

FALSE LABOR

Your mare has been waxing for several days, then late one night seems to go into stage I labor. Your whole family comes out to watch her, but she never progresses to stage II. You should call your veterinarian and have the mare examined to check for problems with her reproductive tract and placenta just in case there's a hidden problem. However, the mare probably got nervous because of the crowd and has "managed" her pregnancy by delaying her labor until she is left alone.

VULVAR DISCHARGE

Here's another scenario in which an owner ignores a warning sign of trouble. His mare has had a red-tinged vulvar discharge for several days, but he never calls his vet about the problem. Then the mare goes into labor. When her water breaks, the fluid looks cloudy, and has a terrible odor — a sure sign of an infection of the placenta (placentitis) which could put the foal at serious risk of infection. Any pregnant mare with a suspicious vulvar discharge (red-tinged or thick and yellow) should be examined by a veterinarian to rule out infection of the placenta or reproductive tract and to start treatment immediately.

"RED BAG" DELIVERY

When the mare goes into stage II of her labor, be alert and watch for a problem called red bag (premature separation of the placenta). If the mare is in heavy labor (lying down and straining), but her water never breaks, a problem exists. Instead of a milky white amnion presenting first, a red velvety membrane protrudes. This signals a "red bag" delivery, a serious emergency because the foal has been deprived of oxygen, due to premature separation of the placenta (the chorioallantois has failed to rupture). Call your veterinarian immediately, but you don't have time to wait for your vet to act.

Open the red bag using scissors and gently pull on the foal, one leg at a time until its shoulders are through the birth canal. The red bag needs to be ruptured and the foal delivered as soon as possible. Continue to pull gently on both legs until the entire body clears the birth canal. Cleaning its nostrils of fluid, stimulate the foal by vigorously rubbing with towels until your vet arrives.

DYSTOCIA

The delivery of the foal seems to be proceeding normally, but then you take a closer look at the first part of the foal to emerge. The foal has it soles in an upward position. This is an indication of dys-

Never pull too hard when assisting a birth.

tocia (difficult birth). Other signs include more than two feet appearing, front feet appearing without a nose following, or too much time elapsing without any progression in labor. Hopefully, your vet already has taught you how to check the foal's position in the birth canal. Put on a long sterile glove and lubricate it before you insert your hand and arm to check the position of the foal. If the foal is in an incorrect position, summon your veterinarian immediately. If at any time the delivery does not appear to be proceeding as normal, or more than 10 minutes have passed with the mare straining, and no signs of front feet or nose, please call in your veterinarian immediately. The mare will need help to deliver the foal.

I CAN'T JUST STAND THERE AND WATCH!

When watching a mare push for all she's worth to deliver her foal, it is very difficult to stand back and not interfere. Like many other people, I am guilty of jumping in and giving a little tug on the foal. However, pulling on a foal can lead to problems, so you must use care. If the delivery is slow going, then gently pulling on one leg at a time is all right. It might help the foal get its shoulders through the birth canal. However, if you pull on both forelegs at the same time, you might create a shoulder lock. Do not have several large people pulling on the foal — you can injure the foal and/or create tears within the mare's reproductive tract if she is not dilated or fully relaxed. Before pulling, always consult professional help first.

BLEEDING FROM THE UMBILICAL CORD

After the foal has been delivered, if the mare jumps to her feet and breaks the umbilical cord prematurely, the blood will gush from the foal's umbilical stump. Tie a knot around the remaining umbilical stump, using umbilical tape to stop the flow of blood. Clean the umbilical stump with your diluted Betadine or chlorhexidine solution. Then call in your veterinarian immediately.

FAILURE TO STAND AND/OR NURSE

The foal should be standing within two hours of its delivery. If three hours have passed and the foal cannot stand even with assistance from you, have your veterinarian evaluate the foal immediately. The foal might have musculoskeletal problems such as contracted tendons or it might be suffering from septicemia, a severe infection, that leaves it too weak to stand.

Other problems include neonatal maladjustment syndrome, when a foal can stand but seems unable or unwilling to nurse. Your veterinarian should evaluate the foal immediately to determine if it needs treatment or a referral to an intensive care facility. I will discuss the problems associated with neonatal foals in more detail in the next chapter.

RETAINED PLACENTA

If the placenta has not been expelled within three hours of foaling, call your veterinarian. This is considered an emergency because a retained placenta left untreated can lead to infection within the uterus (metritis) and subsequent laminitis, so treatment should be prompt.

POST FOALING COLIC, BLOOD LOSS

Mild signs of colic become more severe and/or the mare loses interest in the foal. Your veterinarian should be called to evaluate the mare right away because serious problems should not go untreated. Problems such as a uterine tear or a uterine artery rupture can lead to severe blood loss, shock, and sometimes death. Intensive therapy, such as blood transfusions and intravenous fluids, often is needed to save the mare. Other gastrointestinal problems can occur, such as large colon twists. Do not delay getting prompt veterinary care when any of these problems arise.

CHAPTER 4

Understanding the Newborn

Once the foal is delivered and starts to move about, the bonding process between the mare and foal begins. Many purists will tell you to leave them completely alone. People in favor of imprinting a human's touch will recommend that you jump right in and rub yourself all over the foal. I see problems with both approaches. I have seen too many mares begin to reject their foals because eager owners and friends want to pet and cuddle the foals immediately after they are born. I recommend drying the foal with towels as it rests quietly with its mother. Rubbing helps stimulate the foal in many ways, including its breathing. Rubbing also allows the veterinarian to remain quietly near the foal to evaluate him or her without disrupting the bonding process. Never make loud noises or sudden movements which could startle the mare, especially if she is a first time mother.

After a short rest, the mare will nicker to and nuzzle the foal. The mare will begin to lick the foal and shortly after she will stand. As she stands, she will rupture the umbilical cord at its natural "break point," about one inch below the foal's abdomen. If the cord has not broken off after about 30 minutes, you should break it with your hands. Since this is a job best left for your veterinarian, I do not usually recommend this, but if your veterinarian is not available, then break the cord. The cord should be grasped above and below the breaking point, then twisted and pulled. Do not to pull too hard. You could tear the cord internally, which can lead to internal bleeding or the passage of urine (also called patent urachus). The cord should not be cut, because it could result in bleeding from the stump. After the cord is broken, it should be dipped in a diluted solution of Betadine or chlorhexidine. For more detailed information on umbilical cords, please see the section on umbilical stump care.

AT A GLANCE

- It's important not to interfere in the bonding process between mare and foal.

- A foal should stand within one hour of birth, and nurse within two hours.

- Call your vet if the foal does not appear normal.

- Keep a supply of colostrum.

STANDING AND NURSING

The foal should show a suckle reflex (sticking out tongue and making sucking noises) within 20 to 30 minutes of birth. Most foals can lift their heads and necks within a few minutes of birth. The foal will make several attempts to stand, usually taking several spills in the process. With each try, though, the foal should seem stronger. After the foal makes a few solo attempts to stand, offering a gentle helping hand to steady it is always acceptable. The foal should be able to stand alone within one hour of birth.

Although at first the foal will suckle everything but the mare's

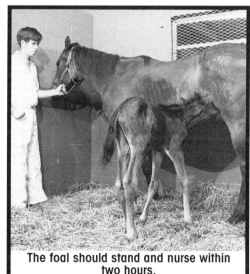

The foal should stand and nurse within two hours.

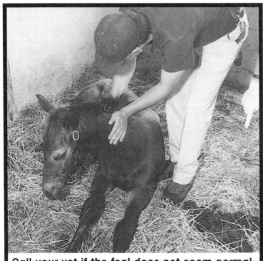

Call your vet if the foal does not seem normal.

nipple, it should be nursing within two hours after birth. Normally, the foal will drink from the mare, then lie down to rest at frequent intervals. This is perfectly normal behavior. It is abnormal for a foal to lie down and stay down for several hours. This indicates a problem. Your veterinarian should be summoned. If the foal does not stand and nurse within three hours or stands, but shows no suckle reflex and/or little interest in the mare, ask your veterinarian to examine the foal immediately. The veterinarian will check for musculoskeletal problems which might be preventing the foal from standing, such as contracted tendons.

Foals suffering from neonatal maladjustment syndrome, called "dummy foals," might not be able to stand or can stand, but wander the stall with little interest in the mare. These foals will not have a suckle reflex. You can check the suckle reflex by placing your clean fingers in the foal's mouth, which should stimulate sucking action. If there is no reflex, have the foal evaluated by your veterinarian.

COLOSTRUM OR "FIRST MILK"

A foal must receive colostrum, or "first milk," within six to eight hours of birth because its gastrointestinal tract can only absorb the immunoglobulins (antibodies) present within the colostrum during a short window of time — usually within 12 hours of birth. Remember, the foal cannot obtain antibodies from its dam before birth due to the impermeable placenta. In many species, the permeable placenta allows for a transfer of disease-fighting antibodies from the mother to her fetus. The foal is born with virtually no ability to fight off infection other than the antibodies it absorbs from the colostrum. Without adequate colostrum, a foal could succumb rapidly to over-whelming infection. Although there might be some nutritional concern when a foal has not ingested colostrum, the temptation to feed it milk, or anything else, during the first few hours should be resisted. Such feeding will hasten the closure of the

Always keep a store of colostrum.

intestinal cells, preventing adequate antibody transfer. If the foal needs nutritional support, it should be administered intravenously until after 36 hours of age. This support should be directed at keeping blood glucose levels normal until milk is ingested. The postpartum mare will produce colostrum for 24 to 36 hours, then the milk will return to a more normal consistency and appearance.

Every farm should have a banked source of colostrum. The colostrum can be saved from mares who drip colostrum early (prematurely lactate), then administered to their foals after birth, either by bottle or naso-gastric tube. Colostrum also can be saved from a mare with a healthy foal. The milk can be frozen and kept for nearly two years. Frozen colostrum can be used when the mare does not produce any colostrum of her own (agalactia) due to illness or fescue toxicity.

If you have a source of frozen colostrum, thaw it in a warm water bath. Microwaving the colostrum on a normal or high setting will destroy the beneficial immunoglobulins within the milk. I always thaw colostrum in a warm water bath. It takes more time (up to an hour), but is safe and I am assured that the colostrum will do its job.

CHAPTER 5

Routine Care of the Neonatal Foal

The newborn foal is an exquisite, yet extremely fragile creature. In this chapter, I'll describe routine care of the foal during the first two weeks of its life, the early neonatal period. Within 24 hours of its birth, even if the foal appears healthy and happy, your veterinarian should give it a thorough examination. I believe it is good management to monitor the foal's basic parameters on a daily basis. This means taking its heart and respiratory rate and its rectal temperature, and observing its activity level and behavior. Obviously, if the foal appears weak or sick, you should call your veterinarian immediately.

CARE OF THE UMBILICAL STUMP

The care of the foal's umbilical stump is a key aspect of neonatal management. I have always likened a foal's umbilical stump to a freeway, a rapid transit system for bacteria to race through the foal's bloodstream. This is why it is so important to keep the mare and foal in a clean stall.

The foal's umbilical stump should be dipped in a dilute solution of povidone iodine (0.1- 1.0%) or chlorhexidine (0.5%) two to three times a day for three to four days. It has been traditional to treat the umbilical stump with tincture of iodine, an alcohol-based solution. In the right strength, tincture of iodine is very effective because it dries the stump while disinfecting it. Three to four percent solutions will accomplish the objectives, while stronger tincture (7%) and the strongest water-based solution (Lugol's solution) could cause excessive inflammation, and, in some cases, predispose the tissues to infection.

AT A GLANCE

• Clean and monitor the umbilical stump.

• A foal should pass meconium within a few hours of birth.

• Administer an enema if the foal does not produce any meconium within a few hours of birth or is straining to defecate.

• Your vet should examine a new foal before it reaches 24 hours of age.

You can use many different kinds of containers to dip the umbilical cord, including a cleaned baby food jar or a large, plastic syringe case (which is my favorite). Just pour the antiseptic into the container, then place it over the umbilical stump covering it completely, and hold it there for a few seconds.

During the first few weeks of the foal's life, the umbilical cord should be monitored at least once a day for any abnormal swelling, moistness, purulent discharge, or the passage of

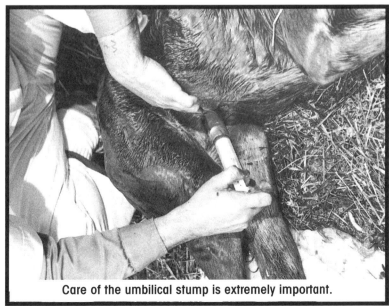

Care of the umbilical stump is extremely important.

urine (patent urachus). If you notice any of these problems, have your veterinarian examine the foal immediately. These abnormalities could indicate a serious infection.

MECONIUM

The meconium is the first manure produced by a foal. Unlike the looser "milk feces" that it will pass later, the meconium is usually hard and pelleted. The meconium is made up of amniotic fluid and other material that the foal swallowed while in the uterus. Most foals will strain to some extent to pass their meconium. Colts more than fillies tend to have a problem passing their meconium. This phenomenon is thought to be related to the smaller diameter of the colt's narrow pelvis compared to a filly's. Usually a foal will begin to pass the meconium within a few hours of birth, and it should be replaced by the softer, yellow milk feces by 24 hours of age. Some foals will not strain at all and pass their meconium with no problems; others will strain and strain and may show signs of colic. I had one foal that never strained, it just began to show signs of colic at two hours of age. I gave the foal an enema, then it produced a large pile of meconium, jumped up, and started nursing. Then 30 minutes later, it began to colic again. Another enema and another large pile of meconium followed, then it went back to nursing. This went on several more times until all of the meconium was gone and the foal began passing softer, fecal matter.

SIGNS OF MECONIUM IMPACTION

The foal assumes a distinctive posture when it strains to defecate. It arches its back and holds its tail up in the air. The foal also might wag its tail back and forth if it is having trouble passing the meconium.

Standard operating procedure on many horse breeding farms calls for giving every neonatal foal a warm, soapy water enema or a commercial enema, like a child-size Fleet's enema, to help ease the passage of meconium. An enema can be administered through a soft rubber tube using a dose syringe. This allows for a gravity flow enema and a larger volume of fluid. If you do not have a commercial enema available, make one by mixing several drops of Ivory soap in a quart of warm water, combined with one cup of mineral oil. (If you do not have mineral oil, substitute one cup of sterile lubricant.) The mineral oil will coat the meconium balls so they will pass easier.

ADMINISTRATION OF AN ENEMA

Giving an enema to a new-born foal should be performed with extreme care. The foal must be properly restrained to lessen the risk of perforating its delicate rectum. Furthermore, the temperature of the fluid being administered must be checked very carefully to avoid scalding the rectum. The temperature should be warm but not uncomfortable on your hand. When your supplies are ready, the foal should be restrained in a standing position. Put lots of lubricant, such as KY jelly, on the nozzle of the enema (or the end of the rubber tubing). Insert the enema nozzle (or tubing) gently. Then squeeze the enema bottle (or begin pouring the soapy water through the tubing).

After you administer the enema, step out of the stall and leave the foal to pass the meconium. Keep watching the foal closely. If it does not produce any meconium or produces meconium but then resumes straining after 30 minutes or so, it is likely that more meconium remains to be passed. If administering a second enema does not produce more meconium or alleviate the signs of distress, then your veterinarian should be called. Some foals develop large meconium impactions and need further treatment, such as mineral oil administered through a naso-gastric tube.

The problem with meconium impactions is that it can produce enough pain to keep the foal from nursing properly. Meconium impactions are not necessarily life-threatening.

But they do require prompt treatment because the meconium can act like a cork in the foal's rectum so that gas and fluids accumulate in the intestines, leading to severe bloat. The bloating can be extremely uncomfortable for the foal. A distressed foal will not nurse properly, and the bloating may also compromise its ability to breathe normally.

Unfortunately, after the foal reaches the severely bloated stage, medical treatment with intravenous fluids and mineral oil will not work fast enough to clear the blockage. Sometimes the young foal will require surgery. Don't wait until it is too late. If your foal has not passed meconium within its first 24 hours, call the veterinarian immediately.

HEALTHY FOAL CHECK

I always refer to the 24 hour vet check as the healthy foal check, mostly because I'm convinced that if the veterinarian hasn't been called in until this time, then most likely the foal

Examining the healthy foal.

is fairly healthy. So why, then, does the veterinarian need to examine a "healthy" foal? If problems occurred during its birth, your veterinarian should have visited the newborn foal before it reached 24 hours of age. Remember, if it appears weak, or if the foal cannot stand, then your vet should make an emergency call no matter what the time of day or night.

During the healthy foal check, your veterinarian will perform a complete physical examination on the foal. This will include taking its temperature, listening to its heart with a stethoscope to determine if there are any abnormalities that might signal a congenital heart defect, and examining its chest for fractured ribs or other problems associated with the lungs. The veterinarian also will look for other congenital problems such as a cleft palate, wry nose, or entropion (rolling in of the eyelids). The foal's musculoskeletal system will be evaluated for angular or flexural deformities (both will be discussed in a later section). The veterinarian will take a medical history by talking to the caregiver who has watched over the foal's first few hours of life. The vet will want to make sure the foal has passed its meconium and is defecating and nursing normally. By evaluating the gamma globulin level, the vet can make sure that the foal has absorbed an adequate amount of immunoglobulins. If not, the vet will give your foal an injection designed to supplement the immunoglobulins, or natural protection that passed from the mare to the foal in her colostrum. Hopefully, no abnormalities will be found and your foal will receive a clean bill of health.

The following pages will describe problems your veterinarian might find on the first day or in the first few weeks of the foal's life.

CHAPTER 6

Neonatal Problems

Remember, just because your foal was born healthy does not mean you are out of the woods. Raising a foal requires close daily observation. This section will describe what the problems look like, what they mean, and what to do about them.

IGG (ANTIBODY) DETERMINATION

The main immunoglobulin (antibody) produced in the colostrum is gamma globulin. There are others produced in smaller quantities. Veterinarians have developed tests to measure the amount of gamma globulins within the foal's blood stream as a way of estimating if an "adequate" quantity of immunoglobulins has been ingested, then absorbed by the foal. Some veterinarians like to perform the test when the foal reaches 12 hours of age, even though the peak level of absorption is 24 hours. If there is a low level of immunoglobulins at 12 to 18 hours, then there is still time to administer more colostrum. If the level of immunoglobulins is low at 24 hours, then the only remedy is administering plasma intravenously. Plasma contains high levels of immunoglobulins, which protect the foal from infection.

There are many different types of tests that can estimate the level of immunoglobulins within the blood stream. Some of the tests can be performed at the farm; others require laboratory analysis. Several on-site tests have a fairly high accuracy level and are an important part of the physical examination of the newborn, as low levels of immunoglobulins can mean the foal is at risk of developing infection. Examples of some of the more common test names are the CITE™ test, FoalCheck™, and a zinc sulfate turbidity test. RID™, a more accurate test, is highly specific for gamma globulins, but the results take 18 to 24 hours.

AT A GLANCE

- Have your vet check the foal's main immunoglobulin before it is 24 hours of age.

- A foal might need more colostrum or plasma if it fails to absorb enough colostrum.

- A foal might need tetanus antitoxin if the mare was not vaccinated.

FAILURE OF PASSIVE TRANSFER

Failure of passive transfer is a syndrome in which foals fail to absorb adequate colostrum. This can result from: 1) the foal failing to ingest an adequate quantity of colostrum; 2) the mare producing colostrum which is lacking in adequate immunoglobulin levels; 3) the mare producing normal colostrum, but prematurely lactating thereby losing the colostrum; 4) the mare failing to produce any colostrum or milk of any kind (agalactia). Regardless of the cause, this syndrome is thought to be the most common predisposing factor of infection in neonates.

Failure of passive transfer can be classified as complete failure or, more commonly, partial failure. In the latter case, some degree of immunoglobulins are transferred from the mare to the foal, but not enough to protect the foal from infection. If the foal is found to have only a low level of immunoglobulins, then your veterinarian will recommend supplementing it with plasma, if available. Whole blood also can be used, but it is not as desirable, because the red cells are not needed except in cases in which the foal is anemic. Whole blood which contains the red cells also can lead to transfusion reactions. Plasma can be purchased commercially. Although it's a bit expensive (about $150 per liter), its contents can save a foal's life.

Just because a foal has a low immunoglobulin level does not automatically mean that it will develop septicemia (a disease caused by infectious microorganisms in the blood). However, the chances are greater than with a foal that has a "normal" amount of immunoglobulins. No one knows exactly what level of immunoglobulins is necessary to protect a foal from septicemia — it varies with the individual animal. However, your vet knows what test range comprises an adequate level. Be aware that it is not uncommon for a foal to be tested at 24 hours of age and found to have a high level of immunoglobulins and still succumb to an infection within the first two weeks of its life. If the bacterial numbers or challenge is great, the foal is more likely to develop septicemia. This is why a clean and healthy environment is so important. Keep the stalls or paddocks clean and free of manure as much as possible, and keep all sick horses separated from the foals. This will help reduce bacterial numbers, and consequently lower the infection rates, on your farm.

VACCINATIONS

Neonates do not require many vaccinations. The routine gamut of vaccinations — influenza, Eastern and Western encephalitis, tetanus toxoid — is not required until six to eight weeks of age. The newborn foal, however, might require tetanus anti-toxin if the mare was not vaccinated with a tetanus toxoid booster during the last few months of gestation. An unvaccinated mare cannot transfer tetanus antibodies to the foal. Consequently, the foal needs protection immediately from the tetanus organism which is found everywhere in the environment.

The vet will probably give the newborn a combination injection of vitamin E and selenium, especially if the mare and foal live in an area that is selenium deficient, particularly if the mare did not receive supplements during pregnancy. Failure to supplement the mare during pregnancy and failure to administer vitamin E/selenium to the newborn could result in the development of White Muscle Disease. The disease could strike the foal at any time up to one year of age. White Muscle Disease is most commonly associated with a deficiency in selenium. Please find out

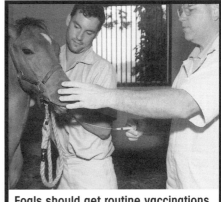

Foals should get routine vaccinations.

from your veterinarian whether you live in a selenium-deficient area. The levels of both substances within the horse can be measured using a blood test, but it takes up to one week to get the lab results.

NEONATAL MALADJUSTMENT SYNDROME

Neonatal maladjustment syndrome is a term used to describe foals which show abnormal behavior or display neurologic abnormalities such as stupor, blindness, or seizures. This syndrome has many names, the most common being "dummy foal," and is thought to be related to a decrease in oxygen (hypoxia) during the birth process. The decrease in oxygen to the fetus can result from many different factors. A few examples include dystocia, premature separation of the placenta, or obstruction of the umbilical cord, which disrupts the blood supply to the foal. Although the causes can be myriad, the result of the hypoxia is thought to be the same — swelling of the brain (cerebral edema). The degree of damage to the brain can produce a variety of clinical signs, including a lack of interest in the mare, wandering the stall or paddock, or very deep sleep from which it is difficult to rouse the foal. More severely affected foals will have convulsions or seizures. The onset of these signs also can vary from immediately after birth to a few days later, when a seemingly normal foal suddenly begins to display abnormal behavior.

Foals with this syndrome often require intensive care, especially those with seizures. Even foals without seizures might require intensive care to ensure that they receive appropriate nutrition. Since most of these foals will not nurse adequately, they often need to be tube-fed. Treatment is aimed at reducing the cerebral edema and protecting the foal against infection. Many foals recover and do not appear to suffer any long-term affects. Foals which are only mildly affected can recover with minimal care. If your foal displays any abnormal behavior, please notify your veterinarian as soon as possible, as early detection and therapy can improve the outcome.

NEONATAL ISOERYTHROLYSIS

Neonatal isoerythrolysis, often referred to as NI, is a condition that affects neonatal foals within the first few days of life. The foals are born normal, then begin to show signs of the disease after ingesting colostrum. NI results in anemia, which occurs when the foal ingests maternal antibodies primed to attack the foal's red blood cells and destroy them. The mare develops these antibodies and concentrates them within the colostrum. This happens when the mare is sensitized to a red blood cell group, usually from a previous delivery. One example is if the foal's blood mixes with the mother's blood during the birth process. The mother, if exposed to a red blood cell group from the foal's blood, which she does not possess, will develop antibodies to those red cells. The next foal born to that mare is at risk of being affected. These foals are born healthy, then can develop sometimes fatal anemia if not treated appropriately.

The clinical signs of NI are lethargy (weakness), decreased appetite, and icterus (yellow color to the mucous membranes). The foal also will have a rapid heart rate, because as the red blood cells are progressively destroyed, then the blood loses its ability to carry oxygen. The heart must pump blood faster and faster to keep up with the body's oxygen demand. A cross match between the foal and mare's blood will determine if the foal has neonatal isoerythrolysis. Your veterinarian also can do a field test mixing the mare's colostrum with the foal's blood to look for a reaction. If positive, then the foal will require a blood transfusion to replace the red blood cells which were lost and no more access to the mare's colostrum.

How to prevent

The incidence of NI in Thoroughbred mares is about 1%, so it is not a terribly common disease, but can be devastating. There are tests that can be performed before the foal is born to reduce the risk. If a mare has had a NI foal, then she should be tested one to two months before she foals to allow enough time to arrange for another source of colostrum. Usually if the mare is delivering her first foal, this disease is not a concern.

Prevention is the best treatment. Talk to your veterinarian about testing your mare against the stallion's blood. Another way is comparing blood typing of the mare and stallion.

If your veterinarian determines the foal is at risk, then the foal will need to have another source of colostrum. In these cases, the delivery must be attended and the foal often muzzled to prevent it from ingesting the mother's colostrum. Colostrum which has been banked from another mare which is negative for the offending antibodies (determined from a blood test) or plasma transfusions can be used to achieve normal immunoglobulins levels. After the mare stops producing the colostrum (at about 24 to 48 hours) then the foal can be allowed to nurse. If plasma is used, then the foal must receive equine milk replacer or another source of equine milk from a bottle or pail or tube fed by your veterinarian until the foal can begin normal nursing. See the section on feeding the orphan foal in

Chapter 8 for an idea of how much milk the newborn requires. Always consult with your veterinarian as well.

ENTROPION

Entropion is a condition of the newborn's eyelid which often goes unnoticed until the foal begins tearing from the affected eye. This is considered a congenital defect but also could be caused by dehydration and/or trauma during birth. Entropion usually occurs in the lower lid, which rolls inward and touches the surface of the eye (the cornea). The eyelash-

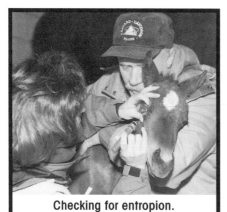

Checking for entropion.

es soon start to scratch the cornea, which could result in a painful corneal ulcer. You might be able to correct the problem by rolling the lid outward with your thumb. If the lid immediately goes back to touching the eye, then your veterinarian will need to suture or staple the lid to keep it from touching the eye. If a corneal ulcer has formed, then the eye will need treatment with topical ophthalmic ointment. The staples or sutures will remain in place (usually two weeks) until the lid no longer tends to roll inward. Entropion is not an emergency, but should be corrected at the 24-hour healthy foal check.

PATENT URACHUS

The urachus is the structure which connects the foal's bladder to the allantoic space. The urachus travels within the umbilical cord along with other structures such as the umbilical veins and arteries. The foal's urine collects in the allantois during gestation. After birth, the urachus should close as soon as the umbilical cord is severed. If at any time, you see urine dribbling or streaming from the urachus, it is considered patent. A patent urachus is easy to determine in a filly but is harder to spot in a colt. It can be difficult to tell whether the colt just sprayed urine from the urethra onto the end of the umbilicus or if the urachus is truly patent. It can often take several close looks.

The urachus can be patent for one of two reasons: 1) the urachus never closed after the umbilical cord broke, a condition known as a congenital patent urachus; or 2) the urachus can open back up after having been closed, usually due to infection of the urachus or infection elsewhere in the body. If you notice that your foal is urinating through the urachus, then call your veterinarian. An examination will determine infection within the umbilical stump/urachus or elsewhere in the body, such as the lungs or gastrointestinal tract.

Treatment of a patent urachus is controversial. Most veterinarians agree that if there is evidence of an abscess or infection within the urachus or umbilical stump then it should be surgically removed to prevent spread of the infection. The controversy begins when discussing whether or not a patent urachus without signs of infection should be removed. Many veterinarians believe that an open (patent) urachus is just a portal for more bacteria to enter the blood stream. Others believe that an acquired patent urachus — one which has opened due to infection elsewhere in the body — is not the source or even potential source of infection and will close on its own as soon as the foal recovers from the infection. In the meantime, the foal is often treated with umbilical dips and/or cauterization of the urachus to encourage it to close.

As an owner, you should be aware that surgery to remove the urachus can have complications. The anesthesia itself is stressful on the foal, especially if pneumonia is present. Surgery can lead to excessive scar tissue formation within the abdomen (called adhesions), which can cause obstruction of the intestines. Sometimes, a second surgery is needed to correct the adhesions. This complication is rare. I have seen two in about 100 operations to remove an infected or patent urachus, but you need to discuss the options with your veterinarian and reach a decision that satisfies you both.

HERNIA (UMBILICAL AND SCROTAL)

Umbilical hernia

An umbilical hernia is an outward swelling or mass in the umbilical area. It results from a defect in the abdominal wall involving the portion of body wall through which the umbilical structures pass. When the vet palpates the area, the swelling should be soft and non-painful and it should be possible to push the bulge back gently into the abdomen (reducing the hernia). Umbilical hernias are usually surgically corrected for cosmetic reasons and because they could entrap a section of intestine, which will cause colic. If the entrapment is severe it could lead to loss of blood supply to the segment of bowel, necessitating resection of that segment. A hernia also might result from the umbilical structures becoming infected. If so, it should be corrected.

Hernias that are less than a few centimeters in length often close spontaneously and usually do not require surgery. Larger hernias are usually corrected surgically when the foal is weaned, unless they are very large (greater than 10 cm) and those should be corrected early in life. If your foal does have a hernia, then monitor it for swelling, pain, and reducibility. If the hernia ever becomes non-reducible, it means the contents are entrapped and surgery should be performed as soon as possible.

Scrotal hernia

A scrotal hernia is also a hernia, but the herniated intestines have gone through a natural slit in the body wall, the one through which the spermatic cord travels. Needless to say, scrotal hernias only occur in colts, or male foals. The natural opening is the inguinal (vaginal) ring and in these foals or adults, the ring is abnormally large and allows the intestines to slip down into the scrotum. The herniated intestine often slips down next to the descended testicle. You will notice these hernias as a soft swelling in the scrotum. With congenital scrotal hernias, the intestine usually does not become entrapped and you can easily push the intestines back into the abdomen.

I often recommend that the hernia be reduced (pushed in) multiple times a day. Eventually, the enlarged ring will close on its own without surgery. However, the herniated intestine can become entrapped, making the hernia non-reducible, or the intestines will burst out of the scrotum. When this happens, it is called a "ruptured" scrotal hernia. In such a case, the intestines are just underneath the skin and the hernia looks quite large. This type of scrotal hernia needs surgery immediately. You should also know that because this type of hernia is congenital, most veteri-

Non-reducible hernias usually require surgery.

narians will insist that the colt be gelded at the time of surgery, in order to prevent passing on of the trait.

CHAPTER 7

Foal Rejection

If a mare rejects her foal, the rejection usually occurs soon after the birth. When the foal begins to move toward the mare looking for milk, the mare runs away. Most of the time, the mare is afraid of the foal and does not try to harm it. Sometimes, the mare will attack her foal. Other times, mares will reject their foals after a prolonged separation.

My first experience with foal rejection occurred when a mare was sent to me for colic surgery. The farm manager kept the six-week-old foal at the farm to prevent its injury during transport because the mare was thrashing around in extreme pain. The owners were not pleased that the mare and foal had been separated, so I asked the farm manager to bring the foal to the hospital after the mare's surgery. The foal arrived three days later. When I put it in the stall with the mare, she tried to remove a large section of the foal's neck as it attempted to nurse. Fortunately, I had put a lead shank on the mare and was able to pull her head away just as her teeth went snap! I knew then that it was going to be a long week.

In this chapter I will focus primarily on the major causes and remedies for foal rejection following delivery, but I will also discuss unusual situations such as the mare who had colic surgery, then treated her foal like a stranger. There are several different manifestations, or degrees of foal rejection.

To understand why foal rejection occurs and how to prevent it, you first must first understand normal post-foaling maternal behavior. I will describe normal behavior between mare and foal, then abnormal behavior, ways to prevent foal rejection, and how to get the mare to accept the foal.

The mare begins to form the bond with her foal during the early stages of labor. At the end of stage I labor, the mare's water breaks and the allantoic fluid which surrounds the foal is expelled. The mare usually

AT A GLANCE

- Foal rejection occurs rarely, but requires immediate human intervention.

- Some mares show aggression toward their foals, but not necessarily rejection behavior.

- Fear motivates some mares to reject their foals.

- Sedation, stocks, or hobbles sometimes can help a mare learn to accept her foal.

spends a fair amount of time sniffing and smelling the fluid. After the mare gives birth, she again will smell the fluid along with the placenta. Initially, she might show more interest in the fluids and placenta than in her foal. The mare also might show flehmen (curling her upper lip) after she smells the fluid. This is considered normal behavior in the mare. Some people believe that this is how the mare recognizes the foal as hers. The mare will identify the foal with both the allantoic and amniotic fluid because the foal will smell like the fluids.

After she has investigated the placenta and fluid fully, she will turn her attention to the foal. First, she will smell the foal, then start to lick it, beginning at the head and moving to the hindquarters. The

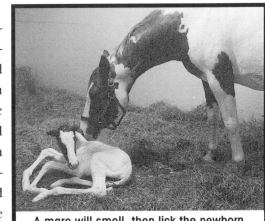

A mare will smell, then lick the newborn.

mare will continue to lick the foal on and off during the first few hours of its life. Other species of animals, including cats, dogs, and cattle, lick their offspring for several days or weeks after birth. This initial touching and smelling experience is crucial for establishing a strong bond between the mare and her foal.

Since the first hour of a foal's life is the most important one in establishing this bond, human contact with the pair should be kept to a minimum unless the mare or foal need veterinary care. As the mother licks the foal, the youngster begins to make attempts to stand. This should occur within one hour of delivery. Foals should begin to nurse from the mare within two to three hours. The mare's first milk or colostrum is of the utmost importance because it contains the immunoglobulins (antibodies) that will help prevent infection in the young foal.

Remember, foals are born with little to no antibodies. If the foal does not ingest the colostrum within three hours of birth, for whatever reason, including the mare's unwillingness to permit nursing, it's an emergency.

NORMAL MARE NURSING BEHAVIOR

In Chapter 4, I described normal nursing behavior of the foal. What is normal behavior for the mare? As the foal nurses, the mare can show a range of normal, even normal aggressive, behavior. Mares might pin their ears, squeal, swish their tails, push the foal away, make smacking noises, and bite or kick at their foals during nursing. This is not necessarily rejection behavior. These examples of aggressive behavior may be a response to pain when the foal bumps against her udder or bites a teat. Although normal, this type of aggressive behavior occurs with more frequency when the foal reaches several months of age rather than with the newborn.

Another normal post-foaling behavior that many people erroneously consider abnormal is aggression of the mare toward humans and/or other horses. This behavior is totally unpredictable until the foal's birth. Even the nicest mare can show dangerous aggression toward humans after the birth of her foal. This behavior is thought to occur instinctively in mares because very young foals instinctively follow any large moving body. So if the mare does not bond properly with the foal, the foal might begin to follow humans or other horses. In the wild, a foal which follows another horse most likely will starve or be attacked by a stallion. So this behavior is understandable in the mare. Remember to approach new mothers with caution and common sense. Aggression toward humans or other horses usually will subside in a few days to one week after birth.

FOAL RECOGNITION

How does a mare recognize her own foal? It is not by vision or smell alone, but through a combination of vision (appearance), smell, and sound. If any of these senses is obstructed (naturally or artificially), it will take the mare longer to identify her foal from others. People use the sense of smell to fool the mare — and to help an orphan foal. For example, if a mare loses her foal and is given an orphan to nurse, the dead foal's placenta can be draped over the orphan foal so the mare will recognize the scent. Placing a product like Vick's Vapor Rub in the mare's nostrils and on the orphan foal also will disguise its scent. This can help in the acceptance process.

MATERNAL BEHAVIOR

Maternal behavior is a complex, instinctive process in most animals. Researchers believe that hormonal influences, genetics, and some learned behaviors can trigger the onset of maternal behavior. Other factors which contribute to maternal behavior include the sight, sounds, and smells of the foal itself. All of these factors come together to induce normal, motherly behavior.

FOAL REJECTION

Foal rejection can be divided into three categories: Avoidance of the foal, rejection of nursing, and actual aggression toward the foal. The first type of abnormal behavior is foal avoidance. This usually involves first-time mothers, otherwise known as primiparous mares. It seems to be a fear-based reaction. The mare will run away from the approaching foal. She usually will not hurt the foal intentionally. However, if they are confined in a small area, such as a small box stall, the mare might accidentally run over the foal or step on it.

A mare which refuses to allow its foal to nurse is an example of the most common maternal behavior problem, according to Katherine A. Houpt, VMD, PhD, a behavior specialist at Cornell University. This problem typically occurs with first-time mothers. Udder problems such as mastitis (inflammation or infection of the udder), which causes swelling and pain in the udder, can lead to this type of behavior. Sometimes, the mare will allow a human to milk her, but will not allow her foal to nurse. If she shows no pain-based reaction when the human milks her, this indicates that it is just the foal's nursing to which she objects.

The third type of abnormal behavior is aggression by the mare toward the foal, which is the least common but most serious. This kind of abnormal behavior is characterized by the mare attacking the foal by kicking or biting its neck and back. The attacks usually come when the foal is standing up and often start when the foal moves close to the mare's food. Most aggressive mares will not attack their foals while they are lying down. The cause of unprovoked aggression is unknown. It seems to be more prevalent in certain breeds. There is some speculation that this behavior actually might be genetic in origin. Arabian mares were the most common breed reported to demonstrate foal rejection in a study by Houpt.

Horsemen know that some mares act aggressively toward their first foal, then settle down to become good mothers in following years. However aggressive behavior can recur with every new foal. Although the mares which show this types of aggression are usually primiparous, those who have rejected two or more foals will probably give a repeat performance the following year.

TREATMENT OF FOAL REJECTION

Prompt human intervention and treatment of any type of foal rejection offers the best chance of reversing the behavior and, most importantly, allowing the foal to ingest colostrum. If the mare will not allow the foal to nurse, she should be milked, and the colostrum administered to the foal by either bottle feeding or through a naso-gastric tube. Your veterinarian will have to do the latter, and should be alerted in any case if the mare shows rejection behavior.

A mare who is frightened of her foal might require sedation to learn to accept it. The veterinarian sedates the mare, who is either placed against a wall in stocks or is hobbled to reduce the possibility of her hurting the foal. The foal is allowed to approach and to nurse. The mare usually learns that the nursing relieves the pressure of her full udder and will soon accept the foal. This method also is used to treat mares which object to nursing.

First, the mare should be examined by your veterinarian to determine if she has any problems which would be causing her udder pain, such as mastitis. If the mare's udder is not painful, then she should be sedated and walked into stocks or restrained using hobbles so that she cannot hurt the foal. At this stage, an experienced horse handler should be present to prevent injury to the foal as the mare becomes accustomed to it. The mare which is aggressive toward her foal will need to be restrained at all times to prevent injury to her foal. Some useful restraints include cross ties, hobbles, or a bar creating a straight stall to prevent the mare from being able to kick the foal or turn sideways. The mare is often sedated just before the foal is first introduced.

Punishment and reward also are used to help the mare overcome her aggressive behavior, but only after the nature of rejection is understood. Obviously, a frightened mare or one displaying rejection due to pain should not be punished. Grain or treats can be fed to the mare while the foal is nursing. If she shows any aggression toward the foal, a whip can be used, but punishment must be given immediately and every time she shows aggression, or other behavior problems will arise.

Dealing with a case of foal rejection requires a great deal of time and effort on the owner's part, because the foal will need to nurse every half-hour around the clock, especially in the first week of life. Furthermore, some mares will not accept their foals, no matter what method is tried.

RETURNING TO INSTINCTS

Maternal behavior is in part instinctive, so if all else fails, give nature a chance. Mares have a strong instinct to protect their foals, especially in the first few days of life. Hence, some mares

Appealing to a mare's instincts sometimes works.

will exhibit normal maternal behavior when the foal is threatened. For example, if the mare and foal are turned out with other horses and another horse shows interest in the foal or the foal approaches another horse, the mare's maternal instincts might be stimulated to guard the foal. If none of these works and the mare will not accept the foal, the foal will have to be raised as an orphan or placed with a nurse mare.

PREVENTION OF FOAL REJECTION

There are a few simple rules you can follow to help decrease the chances of foal rejection. 1) Keep interruptions of the new mare and foal to a minimum unless there is an obvious problem, especially in the first few hours after birth. 2) Avoid introducing strange horses or other unfamiliar animals to the mare's environment for the first few days after foaling. Anxiety over new animals can lead to poor bonding of the mare and foal and possible rejection. For example, do not place a newly arrived horse in the stall next to a mare and new foal or in the same paddock. In the first place, the new horse might be carrying diseases which could make the foal sick and second, if the new horse and the mare do not get along, the aggression the mare feels toward the new horse could become directed at her own foal. 3) If the mare has rejected previous foals, do not re-bed the stall immediately after birth and leave the placenta there for an hour or so. Monitor the mare and make sure she does not try and eat the placenta. If she does, remove it from the stall and save it. Mares do this occasionally, perhaps as an instinctive reaction to the dangers posed by equine predators in the wild.

In my first case of foal rejection, we moved the mare who had colic surgery into a split stall where she could see her foal all the time. We examined her udder for any problems. Then we began sedating and twitching her and allowing the foal to nurse. We allowed the foal to nurse every hour for the first several days. After a few days, the mare did not need sedation or the twitch, and we just held her with a lead line. But we had reached a stalemate. We could not leave them in the stall alone as the mare would bite the foal, especially at feeding time. We decided to appeal to her instincts and turned her out with another mare and foal. It worked like magic. She protected her foal and that ended the problem.

In most cases, mares deliver their foals and accept them without hesitation. However, in the unlucky few cases, rejection poses a serious problem, possibly leading to foal injury or illness. If your mare shows signs of rejection, notify your veterinarian at once.

CHAPTER 8

Orphan Foals and Twins

People who are new to the breeding and raising of horses probably have never experienced the challenge of raising an orphan foal or feeding a foal whose mother is producing little or no milk. The solutions to both problems can be time consuming and somewhat of an ordeal. A foal can become an orphan after losing its mother for a variety of reasons, such as colic or uterine hemorrhage. Or the mother might reject its foal.

Other problems can occur that result in the mare's inability to produce adequate milk for the foal, such as mastitis, metritis (infection of the uterus), and other serious illnesses. If the mare eats certain kinds of fescue grass in late pregnancy, it can block her milk production if the grass harbors a fungus called *Acremonium coenophialum*. Her foal is not an orphan technically, but another source of milk must be found immediately.

In this chapter I will describe raising and feeding orphan foals. I also will discuss the supplemental feeding of foals whose mothers cannot produce enough milk to meet a foal's nutritional needs.

NEWBORN ORPHANS

Newborn foals rely entirely on their mothers' milk for their nutrition. If a foal is orphaned at birth, it is critical to find another source not only of milk, but of colostrum, too. It is imperative that the colostrum be administered as soon as possible because a foal can only absorb the immunoglobulins from the colostrum for approximately 12 hours.

AT A GLANCE

- An orphaned or rejected foal needs colostrum soon after birth.

- Nurse mares are the best solution for orphaned/rejected foals.

- Other, more time-consuming alternatives are bottle and pail feeding.

- Commercial milk replacers are available.

If colostrum is not available, the foal will require intravenous plasma within the first 24 hours of life. Equine plasma contains immunoglobulins to help protect the foal from infection. However, it is expensive, costing about $150 per liter. A 100-pound foal needs between one to two liters of plasma if it has not received any colostrum. If colostrum is available, the newborn foal needs about 250 ml of colostrum every hour for the first six hours, then free choice (but not more than 1 pint, or 16 ounces) every one to two hours.

Your veterinarian should test the foal at 12 to 24 hours of age to determine if it has absorbed adequate levels of immunoglobulins. If its absorption is low, the foal should be given additional colostrum or intravenous plasma as a booster. Otherwise, it will be susceptible to life-threatening infection. Now comes the next problem — how to get the foal to drink.

NURSE MARES

If a foal has been orphaned, a nurse mare provides the best source of milk. The orphaned foal is placed with another mare, who has lost her foal or whose foal has been weaned. Some farms raise mares specifically for this purpose. This might sound like the perfect solution, but there are drawbacks. Nurse mares can be expensive, costing $1,000 or more to lease. Sometimes, the owners of the nurse mare require that you have their mare bred. Secondly, the fostering process can take a lot of time. However, the successful placement of a foal with a nurse mare guarantees the foal a constant food source and ensures proper socialization.

Do not attempt fostering without an experienced person to supervise the introduction process because the mare often requires sedation and/or restraints to prevent it from injuring the foal. The mare should be placed into stocks or hobbled to prevent her from kicking the foal. However, two people are needed at all times while introducing the mare and foal: one to restrain the mare and one to guide and protect the foal. The mare and foal should not be left alone until the mare has fully accepted the foal.

Signs of acceptance include the mare nickering to the foal when the foal is led away and allowing the foal to nurse without resistance. Acceptance of the foal can take several days, or as little as a few hours with a good foster mare.

Nurse mares provide the best source of milk for an orphaned foal.

BOTTLE OR PAIL FEEDING

If a nurse mare is not an option or if the mare rejects the foal, the next alternative is bottle or pail feeding the foal. If the foal has never nursed from the mare, it usually will nurse from the bottle willingly. Lamb nipples are excellent, as they

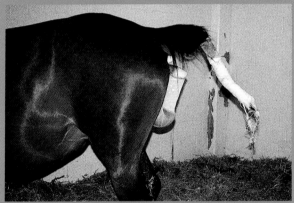

(From top) The mare is in stage I labor, getting up and down and trying to find a comfortable spot; the amnion or white sac covers the two front feet, which have just become visible; the appearance of the foal culminates stage II labor.

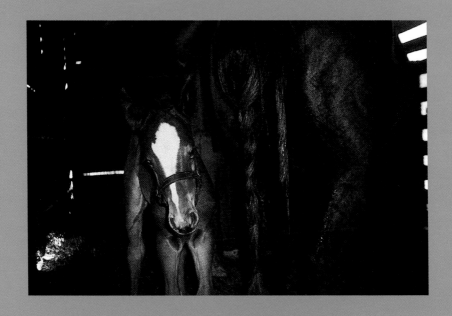

This foal is about six hours old; note the placenta is retained;
(below) a placenta stretched out to make sure it has been
expelled entirely, as has this one.

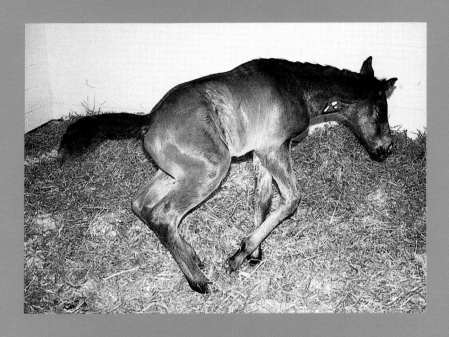

Colic in a two-day-old foal due to a meconium impaction. This foal is demonstrating some typical colic behavior — rolling from side to side and getting up and down frequently.

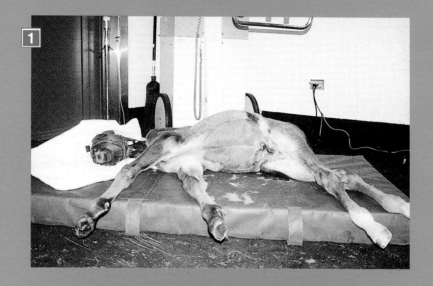

1) A very bloated foal due to a three-day-old meconium impaction;
2) A premature foal receiving oxygen via nasal insufflation and milk
via a stomach tube; 3) A foal with septicemia breathing with help
from a ventilator.

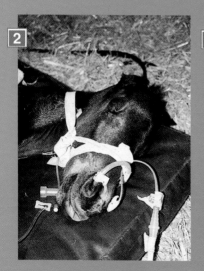

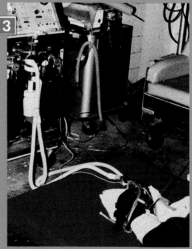

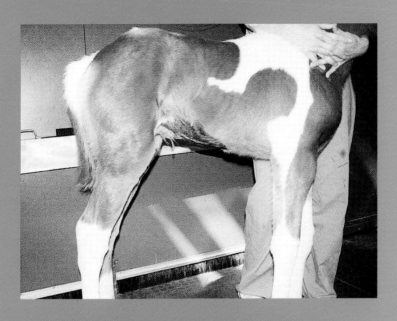

A three-week-old foal (above) with a patent urachus;
(below) a scrotal hernia in a one-day-old Belgian foal.

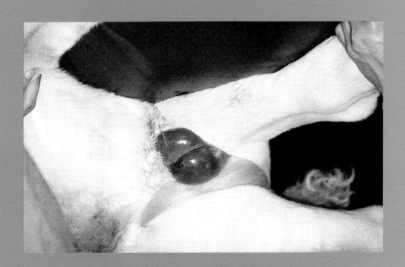

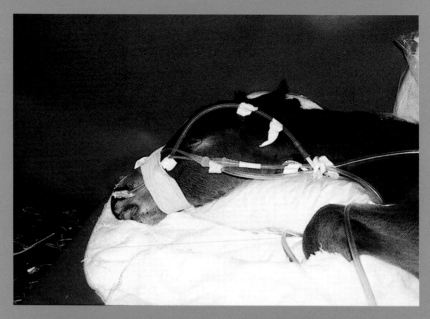

A two-day-old neonate with pneumonia from complete failure of passive transfer; (below) a two-day-old foal born outside in a snowstorm and developed frostbite.

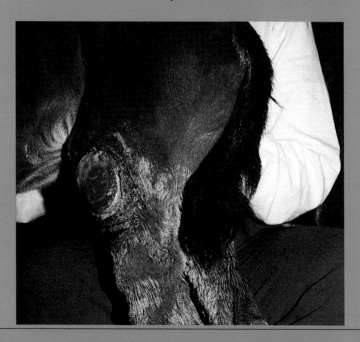

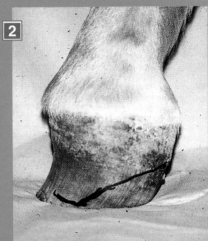

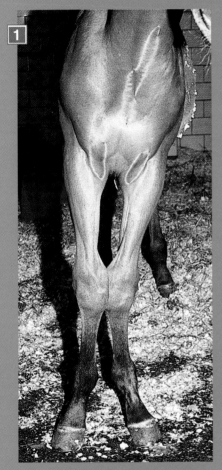

1) A two-month-old foal with angular limb deformities on both front legs; 2) a severely clubbed foot; 3) flexural deformity in the forelegs.

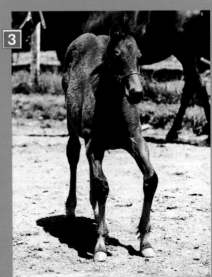

Rarely do both twins live and thrive, but the two above are beating the odds; (below) bottle feeding sometimes is the only solution with an orphan or a foal whose dam does not produce enough milk.

most resemble a mare's teat. If these are not available, Gerber NUK nipples, which are designed for human babies, may be used. Calf nipples are usually too big for foals to nurse effectively. Whichever is used, make sure the hole in the nipple is not too large. When the bottle is turned upside down, milk should not flow out of the nipple, otherwise it flows too fast and the foal could aspirate milk while drinking (inhaling the milk into the windpipe).

A foal fed from a bottle should be placed in an upright position to nurse. This lessens the chance of milk traveling down the foal's windpipe instead of the esophagus, which can lead to pneumonia. To simulate a natural position for nursing, stand with your back to the foal and hold the foal's nose underneath your arm, then gently insert the nipple into the foal's mouth (make sure it's over the tongue). The foal may bump your arm with its head. That is how the foal would stimulate the mare to "let down" her milk. Do not hold the bottle above the foal's head because this position can make it very easy for foals to aspirate

Pail feeding can be an alternative.

milk. Healthy foals usually drink only until they are full, so the foal should be allowed to drink free choice to consume enough colostrum in the first 24 hours.

It is a good idea to record the amount of milk consumed at every feeding, especially in the first few weeks of life, because this can help alert you to a decreasing appetite or developing illness. Remember to clean the bottles and nipples after each use. If the foal has been nursing a mare, then getting it to nurse from a bottle can be quite difficult.

These foals might be more likely to drink from a pail or bucket. Pail feeding is definitely less time consuming and has an advantage as the foal can drink free choice.

Foals usually can be taught fairly easily to drink from a pail. Place milk on your fingers and insert them into the foal's mouth to stimulate the suckle reflex. With your fingers still in the foal's mouth, lower your fingers into a pail of warm milk. Eventually, the foal will get the idea. With this method of feeding, a bucket of mare's milk or milk replacer can be left in the foal's stall or paddock. To avoid the problem of the milk curdling, the milk in the pail should be dumped and replaced with fresh milk every six to 12 hours. The bucket or pail should be hung at chest level for the foal to drink and cleaned every time the milk is changed. Remember, the foal must have access to fresh water at all times.

WHAT TO FEED

The next question is what type of milk should be fed to the foal. Mare's milk is the perfect solution, because it alone matches the nutrient needs of the foal exactly. However, few breeding farms or even equine hospitals have enough milk stored to feed a foal for more than a few weeks. If it's available, it is the first choice. Otherwise, milk from other animals can be used. Cow or goat milk are usually readily available, although neither is the perfect substitute. Cow and goat milk both contain more fat and cow's milk does not contain enough dextrose (sugar). Therefore, if cow's milk is used (2%), then one teaspoon of honey should be added per pint of milk. Goat's milk can be fed without alteration, but is more expensive than cow's milk. Some foals prefer the taste of goat's milk.

Commercial milk replacers also are available. They are a convenient and very acceptable alternative. Several brands specifically formulated to supply the complete nutritional needs of a foal are now available. Whichever brand is used, the replacer should contain approximately 15% fat and 22%

crude protein, so check the label before purchasing. The most commonly used milk replacers for foals used in my area (Northeastern United States) are "Mare's Match," "Foal Lac," "Foal Life," and "NutriFoal." This by no means represents a complete list and other foal milk replacers are perfectly acceptable.

Calf milk replacers have also been used to raise foals successfully. However, many calf milk replacers contain antibiotics, which should never be used in foals. Furthermore, calf milk replacers historically have not contained enough protein for normal growth of the foal. However, the newer brands of milk replacers are more acceptable, but read the product label carefully or talk to your veterinarian before purchasing it. Goat or lamb replacers are also alternatives. But the nutritional requirements for foals are quite different than those supplied by these replacers, especially the ratio of calcium to phosphorus.

While using these kinds of replacers, make sure your veterinarian monitors the foal's growth rate and finds it acceptable. Milk replacers also can cause gastrointestinal upset. Some foals will develop loose stools when the replacers are first used. This is normal, but if the foal develops diarrhea, then the milk replacer should be diluted with water or changed to another brand or type. If the diarrhea persists for more than one day, then your veterinarian should evaluate the foal and institute proper treatment. Sometimes, foals can develop mild bloat (gas) from the milk replacer. If this occurs, discontinue feeding for a few hours then try a more diluted formulation.

Once foals reach one month of age, most are ready for solid feed. A foal will mimic the mare's eating habits and begin to eat grass, hay, or grain with the mare as early as two to three weeks of age. These foals usually are introduced to a creep feed by one month of age. Orphaned foals also should be introduced to grain at this time as well. Feeding milk replacer pellets also can be tried at an earlier age. The pellets usually have to be placed gently into the foal's mouth. Often, the foal will spit them out until it gets the idea.

Starting at one month of age, the foal may be fed small amounts of grain. Newer recommendations for feeding foals include not feeding a high percent protein feed as a creep feed, but the same feed that a weanling would receive (12% or 14%). A good rule of thumb for feeding young horses is one pound of grain per day, per month of age, not giving more than six pounds per day, so a three-month-old foal would receive three pounds of grain per day. Splitting the total amount of grain into two to three feedings also is recommended. This is a guideline only; have your veterinarian check your foal for proper growth and size as some foals will need more and others less grain. Remember, more is not better. Excessive amounts of grain can result in any number of developmental orthopedic diseases in foals such as physitis (abnormal activity in the growth plates), osteochondrosis (including OCD lesions), and flexural deformities.

Foals generally can be weaned from milk replacers by three or four months of age if adequate grass or grass hay and grain is available.

HOW MUCH AND HOW OFTEN TO FEED

A healthy newborn foal will nurse from its dam about seven times in one hour. This number decreases as the foal gets older. As a result, frequent feedings are most compatible with the foal's digestive system. Although calves often are fed only two to three times per day with large volumes at each feeding, this method is not acceptable for foals ingesting only milk. Foals also require anywhere from 21% to 25% of their body weight in milk per day.

The ideal approach is free choice feeding of milk to ensure meeting the foal's requirements. This is quite easy with the bucket or pail feeding method. However, with bottle feeding, the newborn foal will need to nurse every hour for the first few days to one week, then can decrease to every two to three. As you can see, the bucket feeding method has its advantages. The problems arise when the foal is ill and does not consume enough milk. If this happens, your veterinarian should be notified and forced feeding (via a naso-gastric tube) must be instituted.

Sometimes the foal will need to be taken to an equine hospital for intensive care to ensure adequate nutritional support as well as treatment for the underlying illness. In severe cases, intravenous fluids must be administered to correct and prevent dehydration.

But how will you know when your foal is consuming enough milk? Newborn foals should drink about five to seven liters per day in colostrum and milk. Remember, healthy foals need to ingest between 21% to 25% of their body weight in milk per day, so a 75 kilogram foal will need about 19 pints of milk per day. Foals should gain about one to two kilograms of body weight per day. Contact your veterinarian if you are unsure whether your foal is consuming enough milk or not growing properly.

SPECIAL PROBLEMS OF ORPHANS

Raising a foal is a time-consuming job. One main problem with humans raising foals is that the foal will identify with the human species not the equine species. This might be cute when the foal is a newborn, but presents its own set of problems as the foal gets older. Foals raised by people without contact with other horses have been known to show fear of and avoid other horses later in life. One study even showed that foals raised by humans did not learn how to graze properly. Orphaned foals also will try nurse themselves, other foals, or other horses — male or female. These problems can be eliminated by raising the foal with another horse or pony to use as a role model.

Raising an orphan foal can be challenging, but also can result in a healthy, well-adjusted foal. The loss of a mare is not a death sentence for the foal. Raising of an orphan foal, however, should not be attempted without the guidance of your veterinarian.

TWINS

Twin embryos are an unusual and very undesirable phenomenon in the mare. Many other species (cows, sheep, goats) frequently produce healthy twins. But a mare can rarely support twins and carry them to term because of her unique placental attachment to the uterus.

Twins are an unusual phenomenon in horses.

Mares develop twins due to a double ovulation. Both eggs are fertilized and develop into embryos. Twins are a leading cause of abortion in the mare. For those twins born alive, one is usually weaker and dies within a few days of life. Mares which abort twin pregnancies have a

higher incidence of retained placentas, and are often difficult to rebreed during that season. For all of these reasons, veterinarians do not recommend allowing mares to carry twin pregnancies. Mares are examined early in pregnancy (usually around day 14 and 29 post-ovulation) to determine if twins are present. If they are, the veterinarian will determine which procedure to use to eliminate one to prevent loss of both of the embryos later.

Despite the awareness, sometimes twin pregnancies are missed and the mare miraculously carries both fetuses to term. Twin pregnancies should be detected before the mare foals as the birth can be difficult and require veterinary assistance. Furthermore, mares usually cannot produce enough milk to support both foals, and preparations should be made to help care for them.

Mares carrying twin foals will be much larger than mares carrying one foal and they often will deliver the foals early, so monitoring should begin before the last month of gestation. Monitoring the mare for early udder development and lactation is crucial. If the mare was not evaluated by ultrasound early in the pregnancy, then trans-abdominal ultrasound can be performed by your veterinarian in an attempt to determine if twin fetuses are present.

If both foals are born alive, they will need special attention. Twins are usually born smaller than single foals and often they do not survive the first few days. Your veterinarian should be summoned immediately to determine if they are healthy or if either requires treatment to help the chances of both surviving. If the foals are premature or dysmature, they might need intensive care.

Twins foals also will require nutritional support in the form of supplemental feedings. Most mares will not be able to produce enough milk for both foals, so after the colostrum is ingested, then pail feeding with milk replacer should be instituted to give the foals adequate nutrition. Twins also should be evaluated for adequate absorption of immunoglobulins, and supplemental colostrum or intravenous plasma administered if needed. Many twin foals will have musculoskeletal problems in the form of angular or flexural deformities.

Twin foals can be raised successfully, but it usually takes cooperation and hard work between the veterinarian and owner or caregiver.

CHAPTER 9
Flexural and Angular Limb Deformities

I'll never forget the night I received a phone call from a very unhappy man about his three-day-old foal. He said the legs weren't made right and he wanted reassurance that euthanasia was the right solution. I couldn't give him an opinion without examining the foal, but he said his veterinarian already looked at it and three days of physical therapy had not improved the problem. I eventually convinced the man to bring the foal into the clinic. Although the foal had trouble standing on its own, I thought we might be able to help him. The foal's fetlocks and coffin joints were badly flexed, but we custom made splints out of PVC pipe. This helped tremendously, but he needed a little more help, so we per-

Every owner wants a foal with good legs.

formed surgery to cut the check ligaments. This did the trick and the foal went home with new legs. The foal is perfect today and the owner is very happy.

Flexural or angular deformities can be very shocking and even disturbing in severe cases, but appropriate veterinary care offers great hope for these foals. Flexural deformities can be classified into two categories. The first is flexor tendon laxity, which causes the neonatal foal's fetlocks to drop. The second type is flexural contractures, which is flexion of any of the lower limb joints.

AT A GLANCE

- Special shoes or trimming can correct flexor tendon laxity.

- Contracted tendons can be congenital or acquired.

- Evaluate young foals daily to ensure they do not develop contracture.

- Rapid growth can lead to angular limb deformities.

- Proper timing is key to treatment.

FLEXOR TENDON LAXITY

Flexor tendon laxity usually occurs in newborn foals, but can occur in slightly older foals. This laxity can range from a slight drop in the fetlock to the fetlock(s) actually touching the ground. Flexor tendon laxity is common in premature or dysmature foals. This doesn't necessarily mean that if your foal has lax tendons, that he/she is premature/dysmature. Mild laxity usually resolves on its own as the foal gets stronger and exercises — often within a few days to one week. If the laxity is more pronounced, then hoof trimming to create a flat, weight-bearing surface is very beneficial.

Cases of severe laxity require more care, and the foal should be evaluated by your veterinarian. First, the foal's lower limb (heel, pastern, and fetlock) must be protected when it moves or bruising and wounds can develop, which only create another site for infection to develop. Bandaging the lower leg before turn out or hand walking is imperative because sores can develop even on a soft surface. Make sure that the foal is kept in a well-bedded environment when in a stall; clean wheat straw is ideal. Second, if trimming does not help get the foal's heels off the ground, then special shoes are required. These special shoes are usually some form of shoe with a heel extension. My favorite is a glue-on shoe with a heel extension. These shoes stay on well even when the foal exercises. Foals should not wear these shoes for more than two weeks at a time or hoof contracture could develop. Other options include gluing small pieces of plywood to the hoof. Small foals such as miniatures can be treated with tongue depressors glued together, then taped or glued to the hoof. Treatment usually succeeds once the heels are elevated, but it helps for the veterinarian and farrier to have a good working relationship.

FLEXURAL CONTRACTURES

Flexural contractures are often referred to as "contracted tendons." This is because when the affected foal stands, it

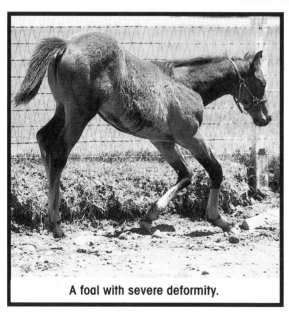

A foal with severe deformity.

appears that the tendons are tense and too short, but this isn't a complete explanation of the problem. This deformity can be present at birth (congenital) or develop in the older foal (acquired). The source of this problem in the newborn is not completely understood, but thought to be caused by malposition of the foal within the uterus. However, nutritional abnormalities and even genetics have been implicated as some mares produce multiple foals with flexural deformities.

Flexural contracture results in the flexion of the joints of the lower limb(s). The joints most commonly affected are the carpus, fetlock, and coffin joint. One or multiple joints or legs can be affected. Flexural deformities also can occur in older foals, known as an acquired flexural deformity. Treating this type of deformity depends on the severity. Mild cases of flexural deformities can resolve on their own with light bandages and exercise. Moderate cases might need splinting and/or casting with the hoof exposed, called tube casting.

Treatment with Oxytetracycline (an antibiotic) has been used with a fair amount of success in relaxing the tendons, but requires caution because of the potential toxic effects to the kidney. Surgery also might be required to help the foal's legs return to normal. Severely affected foals, especially those which cannot stand because joint(s) are fixed in position, might have other congenital birth defects such as spinal cord disorders. Euthanasia is the best alternative in these cases.

FLEXURAL CONTRACTURES — ACQUIRED

These types of contractures occur in older foals and in fairly specific locations. Young foals (one to six months) might develop contracture at the coffin joint. Older foals (at least three months as well as yearlings and occasionally two-year-olds) might develop contracture at the fetlock joint. These contractures occur in the forelegs, usually in both (bilateral), except for cases where the contracture in one leg is due to lack of use because of pain. The cause is not completely understood and is thought to be related to over nutrition (excessive carbohydrate and/or protein content) and/or mineral imbalances. Treatment depends on the severity of the disease, but should begin as soon as possible.

"CLUB FOOT"

Acquired flexural deformity of the coffin joint is often referred to as "club foot." The foot can vary from a dished appearance with the heel raised to a boxy shape with the hoof wall nearly perpendicular to the ground. In very severe cases, the foal or horse might walk on the front (dorsal) aspect of the hoof or fetlock. Mild cases might require only a decrease in nutrition; in young foals weaning might work. Hoof trimming, along with a shoe with an extended toe, might be necessary.

If this conservative therapy does not work, then surgery to cut the inferior check ligament is warranted and often successful. Severe cases often do not respond well to treatment, including surgery, unless the entire deep digital flexor tendon is cut, which is a salvage procedure only. The prognosis for athleticism in these cases is guarded. The key is beginning treatment early. A delay in treatment or diagnosis can lead to undesirable results. Young foals should be evaluated on a daily basis to ensure that they are not beginning to develop contracture or other developmental orthopedic diseases.

ANGULAR LIMB DEFORMITIES

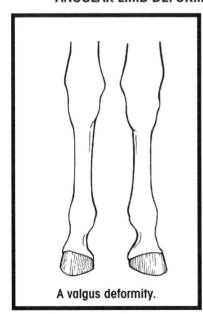

A valgus deformity.

Angular limb deformities are deviations which occur from side to side, such as when the leg deviates from the carpus, tarsus, or fetlock to the outside (laterally) or inside (medially). A lateral deviation is called a valgus deformity and a medial deviation is called a varus deformity. These deviations are extremely common and can be congenital (present at birth) or acquired (develop later in the foal's life). There are several primary reasons angular deformities occur:

• Unossified carpal and tarsal bones due to prematurity or dysmaturity.

• Laxity in the soft tissues surrounding a joint and muscles.

• Abnormal uterine positioning.

• Uneven growth at the physis (growth plate) of long bones.

• Rapid growth.

• Trauma.

A physical examination by the veterinarian as well as radiographs will help determine the cause. Radiographs (X-rays) allow for evaluation of the bones to ensure that they are formed completely. Radiographs also allow for documentation of the degree of angulation. Many foals, especially Thoroughbreds, are born with a mild angulation to both carpi and this usually will correct spontaneously during the first month of life.

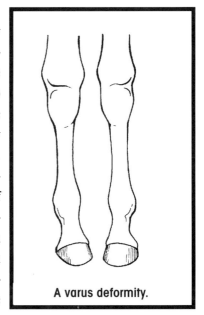

A varus deformity.

But what about more severe deformities?

TREATMENT

Soft tissue laxity can lead to some very severe deformities. These types of deformities are most easily corrected with the use of tube casting, which allows the foot to be exposed. These casts keep the affected joints in a normal position until the soft tissue structures become stronger and can support the joint.

Unossified carpal or tarsal (hock) bones also are treated by tube casting. Without cast support, the incompletely formed bones cannot bear the weight of the foal and literally can become crushed, which is referred to as carpal crush or tarsal crush syndrome.

SURGICAL TREATMENT

If the angular deformity does not correct on its own within a few weeks or is moderate to severe, then surgical therapy should be attempted. Surgery to treat these deformities involves one of two procedures. Periosteal elevation helps stimulate growth. The procedure is used when there is uneven growth and one side of a long bone is growing at a faster rate than the other, leading to an angular limb deformity. This procedure involves making an incision in the periosteum (the covering of the bone) on one side of the bone. This is a rather simple surgical procedure, has little risk involved, and good cosmetic results. Many times, this procedure will be performed early in a foal's life, even on those with only mild deformities, just to ensure that the leg(s) become straight.

The second type of procedure is called transphyseal bridging. This involves placing screws and wires or orthopedic staples to slow growth on one side of a growth plate. This is used for moderate to severe deformities. The procedure's disadvantage is that the implants (screws and wires or staples) must be removed during a second operation.

The foal requires close monitoring as the implants, if left in place too long, actually can cause the foal to over correct, leading to a angular deformity in the opposite direction. The implants must be removed as soon as the leg is straight.

The trick with angular limb deformities is timing. Angular limb deformities, even severe ones, can be corrected, but the foal must be treated at the appropriate time for that joint. Improper timing can result in a residual deformity, which might decrease the foal's value as a sale yearling or lead to early joint degeneration due to abnormal loading. Deformities of the carpus and hock should be corrected within four months of life. However, most corrective surgeries are performed between two and four weeks of age to ensure correct conformation.

Deformities of the fetlock are much more critical as the rapid growth phase is much shorter in this area, therefore not allowing as much time for correction as in the carpus or tarsus. These deformities should be addressed by one month of age. It is always tragic to see a beautiful weanling whose conformation was ignored until preparations get under way for sale. By then, it is just too late. Have your veterinarian evaluate your foals early. Correct conformation goes a long way in preserving soundness in any discipline.

CHAPTER 10
The First Week

The first week of life is one of the most exciting for an owner and for the foal, or so it seems. During the first week, the foal will continue to explore its new environment as it gains strength. The owner or handler can lay the groundwork for training by getting the foal accustomed to handling, wearing a halter, and following the mare. Handling the foal in the early stages of its life could prevent the anxieties and potential injuries that might occur when handling is attempted later. Monitoring the foal for any signs of disease should occur throughout the first week as neonates remain at risk for infection. Again, I feel it is a good idea to monitor the foal's basic parameters (temperature, heart rate, and respiratory rate) once a day if possible during the first week of life. This will allow you to become familiar with your foal's vital signs and get the foal used to being handled. It also can alert you to early signs of illness. If your foal is sick, your veterinarian can begin treatment early. The rest of this chapter will cover basic management concerns of the newborn foal.

TURN OUT

Mares and foals enjoy being turned out and it is an excellent source of exercise for both of them. I think it is wise to leave the mare and foal confined to a box stall for 24 hours until the foal is strong enough to follow the mare at a trot or gallop. This can take two or three days if the foal has been ill or has musculoskeletal problems which preclude exercise. Once the foal is strong enough, it should be turned out with the mare alone, at least for the first few days. Keeping the pair separated from other horses can prevent injury in the event of an overly protective mare or overly curious foal.

The paddock should be clean and free of objects that could

> ## AT A GLANCE
>
> • One hour of turn out per day is sufficient for young foals.
>
> • Early handling makes working with foals easier in the long run.
>
> • Use milk supplements if the mare does not produce enough milk.
>
> • Foal heat diarrhea usually occurs at six to 10 days of age.

hurt the foal, such as farm equipment, hardware, or other debris. The other factor in turn out is the weather. Young foals should not be turned out if it is cold and wet. The neonate cannot keep its body warm for long periods in adverse weather, and frostbite is a real concern. If it is rainy and cold, keep your foals inside. However, foals do well on sunny days in the snow. Snow offers a better footing than mud, so turn out is fine for an hour or so. If you live in a warmer part of the world, turn out in a dry paddock is always good. Many people in colder climates turn out their mares and foals individually in small indoor rings or covered round pens. With the soft footing, they make an excellent alternative to outdoor paddocks.

Foals in the first week of life need to be monitored while outside to make sure they do not become tired and lie

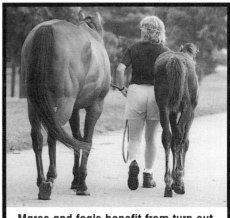

Mares and foals benefit from turn out.

down in the mud or snow. One hour of turn out per day often suffices for foals of this age.

HALTERING AND HANDLING

The best time to begin handling a foal is when it is small. Gentle handling during this stage can save hours of frustration later. The newborn can begin wearing a halter within the first few days of life. Just make sure the halter fits properly. A foal wearing a loose halter runs the risk of getting its foot caught in it. With a properly fitting halter, you should be able to place two fingers underneath the jaw comfortably. Remember, the halter will need to be adjusted or replaced with a larger halter on a weekly basis as the foal grows or rub sores can occur. I also prefer leather halters to nylon halters if the halter is to be left on all the time. If the foal becomes caught, leather halters will break much easier than nylon halters. Foals can injure themselves quite severely if left to struggle in a caught halter.

Start handling foals early.

Handling can begin with gently restraining the foal by placing your arms around it. One arm should go across the chest of the foal and the other should gently lift the tail in the air. Do not pull on the tail — just lift upward from the base. This usually will immobilize a newborn foal, so that a physical examination can be performed, blood drawn, or bandages applied. Older foals also might need to be placed against a wall to be restrained in this manner.

While restraining foals younger than two weeks of age, never pull against the halter or attempt to restrain a foal by the halter. Furthermore, never attach a lead shank and attempt to restrain a foal of this age by the lead. This could result in disaster. Healthy foals often will pull or rear against this type of restraint, sometimes flipping over backwards. Flipping can have disastrous consequences — from blindness, to broken cervical vertebrae (necks), or any other number of broken bones in the legs or skull.

When the foal becomes accustomed to following its mother to and from the turn-out area (this should only take one or two days), then it is a good idea to begin using a butt rope. A butt rope is some type of soft cotton lead that goes around the foal's butt and is held at the withers. Pressure on the rope will encourage the foal to move forward. Moving the mare away from the foal usually will prompt the foal to move forward as well, so this in combination with the butt rope should help the foal learn quickly. The cotton lead can be attached to the halter and still used as a butt rope, offering an early lesson in leading. The handler should always remain patient during this process.

FEEDING

Feeding of a foal during the first week only becomes a concern if the foal is an orphan or if the mare is not producing enough milk. If you have an orphan foal, please read the chapter about orphans. If the mother is producing enough milk, then the foal can acquire all its nutrition from mother's milk during this time. Foals usually become curious and begin to eat hay and share their mother's grain within the first few weeks of life, but milk delivers all their nutritional needs. How do you know if your mare is producing enough milk? Excellent question. I think the best way to tell if a foal is receiving enough milk is to watch the foal and check the mother's udder for milk production. Let me explain. First, a neonate will nurse up to seven times an hour. Foals need frequent small meals. As they approach their mother's udder to nurse, they often "butt the bag" or knock the udder with their heads to stimulate milk let down in the mare. After the foal nurses, it will lie down and nap. Then the foal will wake up and nurse and play a bit before sleeping again. If a foal is not receiving adequate milk from its mother, it will constantly butt its mother's udder. The foal might nurse, but will not lie down and sleep and will act restless.

The other parameter to monitor is the mother's udder. A mare producing adequate milk often will stream milk after the foal butts the udder, and you actually can milk the mare to gauge how much milk she is producing. If you can milk only a few ounces from the mare, she might not be producing enough for the foal. However, if you can milk several pints in one milking, then she has plenty of milk. Ultimately, the foal's condition will tell you if it is receiving enough milk, but you don't want to wait until you notice that your foal is quite skinny to begin supplementing.

Supplementing milk is necessary if the mare is not producing enough milk, either due to illness or fescue toxicity. Supplementing the foal can be done by using the pail feeding method with any of a number of good quality equine milk replacers.

Training the foal to drink is usually quite simple, especially if the foal is hungry. I usually start by placing milk on my fingers and having the foal suck on my fingers, then guiding the foal to the milk pail and placing my fingers in the milk while the foal is sucking on them. This has worked most consistently for me. Foals can receive milk replacer two to four times per day depending on how much supplementation is necessary. Your veterinarian can help make that determination. The beauty of this type of feeding program is that it is simple and requires very little of your time.

This was best exemplified to me as a veterinary student when we visited a farm in northern Georgia where a mare had produced very little milk following her foal's birth because of fescue grass ingestion. The foal was three weeks old at the time of our follow-up visit. The mare and foal were in a large paddock when we arrived at the farm. The owners wanted us to see how they were feeding the foal. I was amazed that after the owner mixed up the milk replacer and walked out to the gate, the foal came running toward them, stopped, drank the replacer, and ran back to join his mother. The foal was growing normally and was very healthy, but had required multiple plasma transfusions and antibiotics shortly after birth due to the lack of colostrum production.

Most foals not getting enough to eat will require milk supplementation until they are six to eight weeks old, at which time they can be weaned onto solid feeds. If you have a question about your mare's milk production, have your veterinarian examine your mare and foal as soon as possible.

FOAL HEAT DIARRHEA

Foal heat diarrhea usually occurs at six to 10 days of age, and corresponds to the same time as when the mare is experiencing her first heat cycle after delivery. The foal will have loose feces (diarrhea or scours), but will remain bright, nurse well, and show no ill effects from the diarrhea. The diarrhea usually resolves in a few days. Veterinarians think the cause of this diarrhea is due to a change in the flora (normal bacteria) within the gastrointestinal tract and is not related to the heat cycle of the mare as orphan foals also experience "foal heat diarrhea." Foals of this age also are susceptible to other causes of diarrhea, so the foal must be monitored carefully. Diarrhea from other causes often will result in a fever, and the foal will become depressed, lose interest in nursing, and/or become dehydrated. If any of these signs are present, have your veterinarian examine the foal immediately as this is not typical of foal heat diarrhea. The diarrhea can result in feces scalding the foal's hindquarters, so cleaning the backside once or twice a day with a gentle soap, then applying petroleum jelly, Desitin, or Vitamin A and D cream will do a lot to help prevent hair loss and irritation.

CHAPTER 11

The First Month and Beyond

The first month in a foal's life is a critical time. Once a foal has made it through the delicate neonatal period, then it's time to start considering other aspects of foal management. When a foal reaches four weeks of age, the owner or caretaker has to consider whether to begin feeding solid feed (creep feeding) and how to handle such problems as persistent angular limb deformities or persistent hernias (scrotal/inguinal or umbilical).

FEEDING

During the first month of life, the foal will begin to eat solid food. Many foals will begin to chew on hay and share their mother's grain within the first few weeks. Once foals have reached the end of the first month, I think they can begin to eat solid food. As mentioned earlier in the book, nutritionists are beginning to recommend feeding a lower percent protein grain, such as weanlings get (12% to 14%), rather than a creep type feed. This can begin at the end of the first month, although some people prefer to wait until the foal is three months old. Talk to your veterinarian. Feeding grain might be necessary for a foal whose mother does not produce enough milk to sustain it at this age. If the mother's milk is very rich and profuse, then the foal might benefit from waiting until it is older to receive grain, as too much protein can induce acquired flexural deformities, physitis, or other developmental orthopedic diseases. Remember, the general guidelines for feeding: one pound of grain per day/per month of age until six months.

After your foal has been eating grain for a couple of weeks, have your veterinarian determine whether the foal is receiving an adequate amount. Clean, mold-free hay is always good for mares and foals, and if you feed alfalfa, then much less

AT A GLANCE

- Foals can begin eating solid food after the first month of life.

- Good hoof care must not be overlooked.

- Some limb deformities might require surgery.

- Start foals on a vaccination schedule at about three to four months.

grain will be required. As for the broodmares, if you live in a selenium-deficient area, then a daily supplement of vitamin E/selenium might be necessary.

The feed can be placed within a "creep feeder" or feed tub that has bars across it to prevent the mare from being able to gain access to the foal's feed. Otherwise, the mare often will eat her grain as well as the foal's. Bars also allow the foal to eat the grain free-choice.

ANGULAR LIMB DEFORMITIES

Limb deformities were discussed in detail in another section. All of the foals should be evaluated at four weeks of age by an experienced veterinarian to determine if corrective measures need to be taken. Foals with angular limb deformities might need only trimming or corrective shoeing to resolve the problem. Others might need surgery. One type of surgery is periosteal stripping, which involves making an incision on one side of the periosteum of the affected long bone. One of the theories about how this procedure works is that release of the periosteum stimulates bony growth. This surgery is minor, quick, and comes with very little risk. A

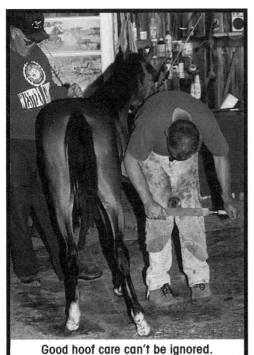
Good hoof care can't be ignored.

more invasive procedure for severe angular deformities or for foals with little growth potential left is transphyseal bridging. This procedure involves implanting orthopedic staples or screws and wires to close one side of the growth plate (the area of the long bone from which the bone grows), enabling the other side of the leg to "catch-up" and straighten.

Transphyseal bridging increases the risk of infection and can leave cosmetic blemishes. This type of procedure also requires two surgeries: one to place the implants and one to remove them. The foal also must be monitored diligently for when the affected leg is straight, then the implants must be removed, or overcorrection can occur.

HOOF CARE

Another aspect of foal management that too often goes ignored is good hoof care. Some people overlook hoof care because foals are usually not forced to exercise (riding, lunging, etc.). Foals which spend a lot of time outdoors will keep their hooves worn down to a certain extent. But all foals need to have their hooves trimmed regularly. Foals with abnormally shaped hooves or those with rotational or angular limb deformities require trimming every three to four weeks to correct their problems. If you are unsure, ask your veterinarian and farrier. Furthermore, teaching the foal to stand for a hoof trim will only make future farrier work less stressful.

NORMAL BEHAVIOR

Throughout the first month, the foal will continue to remain very close to its mother. During the first week, foals will nurse as often as seven times per hour. By the end of the month, the nursing frequency will decrease significantly to three to four times per hour as the foal begins to consume feed from other sources. Foals also might be seen to eat their mother's feces. Known as coprophagy, this behavior is quite normal and cannot be prevented. Many veterinarians think that foals acquire nutrients and/or bacteria necessary for their gastrointestinal tract by eating their mother's fresh feces.

THE SECOND MONTH AND BEYOND

The next step in raising a healthy foal is preventing diseases through vaccinations. Vaccination schedules for foals recently have come under scrutiny by veterinarians. We will discuss the options and recommendations for vaccinating foals. Other management concerns at this time are deworming and hoof care, often overlooked in youngsters.

VACCINATIONS

Vaccinating the foal is an important part of its health management. The maternal antibodies acquired from the colostrum will protect the foal for the first eight to 12 weeks of life, then begin to fade. At this time, it is important to begin stimulating the foal's immune system with vaccines. However, it has been noticed recently that vaccinating foals early is not beneficial and can give a very false sense of security. The problems arise when foals receive vaccinations and they still have maternal antibodies present. The maternal antibodies will interfere with the vaccination and prevent a proper immune response. Therefore, new recommendations for foal vaccination strategies are being initiated to ensure a proper response. Vaccinations recommended for foals include tetanus, influenza virus, Eastern and Western en-

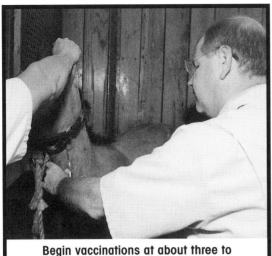

Begin vaccinations at about three to four months of age.

cephalitis, rhinopneumonitis (EHV-I), and in some areas rabies and Potomac horse fever. The American Association of Equine Practitioners recommends that foals not receive vaccinations until they are three to four months of age, then get monthly boosters for two months. The tetanus toxoid and rabies vaccines can be given once at three to four months of age, followed by one booster in four weeks.

For farms with high-risk situations (large populations of foals or farms with recent outbreaks of disease), then foals can begin vaccinations at two months of age, with monthly boosters until six months of age, followed by boosters at nine and 12 months. Hopefully, these vaccination schedules will maximize the chances of preventing infectious disease outbreak on your farm. Remember, however, that vaccines alone cannot prevent disease. Isolating new and infected horses and sanitizing areas exposed to infectious organisms are important as well.

DEWORMING

Deworming programs are just as important for foals as for adult horses. When should a foal begin deworming and with what product? I recommend deworming (not worming) at six weeks of age, then continuing on a program of deworming every eight weeks. All of the commercially available dewormers (paste dewormers) are quite effective, but rotation of major classes (not just brand names) of dewormers is still advisable every other month. I also recommend deworming all young horses with a double dose of Strongid paste once a year (usually in the fall) to rid them of tapeworms which have been associated with intussusceptions (when one section of bowel telescopes into another section). Veterinarians think that the tapeworms

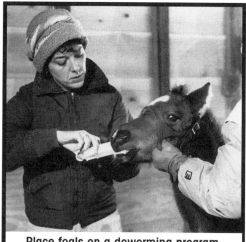

Place foals on a deworming program.

might alter normal motility of the bowel, predisposing intussusceptions. Always consult with your veterinarian to decide what deworming program is appropriate.

CHAPTER 12

Foal Pneumonia, Septicemia, and Diarrhea

Foals can be particularly prone to developing pneumonia, and it is a major concern on most breeding farms with large populations of horses. Foals are susceptible at all ages, so the disease poses a constant threat. Pneumonia can develop insidiously with no obvious, outward signs until it has reached the advance and terminal stages.

In this chapter, I will discuss the common causes of pneumonia (bacterial pneumonia), what signs to look for, and tips on how to prevent pneumonia from decimating your farm.

WHAT IS PNEUMONIA?

Pneumonia, as most people know, means disease involving the lungs. The actual definition is inflammation of the lungs, which could be due to a multitude of factors, bacterial pneumonia, viral pneumonia, etc. Pneumonia was found to be the major cause of illness and death in foals from one to six months of age, according to a Texas A&M study. A Canadian report found that 75% of foals on Thoroughbred breeding farms in that area developed pneumonia. Many foals develop pneumonia that goes undetected, the disease resolves on its own, but is transmitted to other foals on the farm without us knowing. That's the danger with pneumonia in foals; certain bacteria can cause huge outbreaks on farms and affect the majority of the foal population.

Foals which are in the early stages of pneumonia might show no obvious signs of disease. The more subtle signs of pneumonia include an increased respiratory rate (tachypnea) and/or increased respiratory effort. Foals with more advanced pneumonia might have a fever, nasal discharge (purulent material or pus coming from both nostrils), and/or coughing. Unfortunately, these obvious signs are not always present, even in very sick foals. Nasal discharge might or might not be present as the discharge often is swallowed. Foals with severe pneumonia will have marked respiratory effort — the foal might look like he is breathing as if he had just finished a race. Foals which are this sick often are misinterpreted as having colic because they are in such a state of distress.

> ## AT A GLANCE
>
> • Pneumonia is a common and sometimes fatal disease.
>
> • Pneumonia can be so subtle that it might go undetected until it is too late.
>
> • Weak foals could be suffering from septicemia.
>
> • Diarrhea can have many causes and be contagious.

Other signs of illness (not just pneumonia) in foals can include lethargy (not as active or playful as normal). Sick foals also might not eat or nurse as much as they should. You might notice that the foal's head is covered in milk due to its weak attempts at nursing. A sick foal will go to the udder and bump the mare's bag, stimulating milk letdown, then just stand under the udder while the milk streams all over his face. Monitoring the mare's udder also is a telltale sign of foal well-being. If the mare's udder is engorged, and occasionally streaming milk, the foal is not nursing. A healthy foal will nurse from the mare six to seven times an hour, keeping the udder small.

The best way to monitor your foal is to watch for any signs of coughing or nasal discharge — these are the hallmark signs of pneumonia. You also should become familiar with the normal resting respiratory rate and character of breathing for your foals. Neonates (foals less than two weeks of age) often

Pneumonia in a weanling.

have resting respiratory rates of 30 breaths per minute. Older foals (one to six months) often have respiratory rates much lower at 12 to 24 bpm. These rates can change if the weather is very hot and humid or if they have just been running or playing. But, if your foal's respiratory rate is higher than it should be for no reason, have your veterinarian examine the foal.

Being able to detect subtle changes in your foal's breathing requires skill. Watch for flaring of the nostrils and increased movement of the rib cage when breathing. If your foal is displaying these signs while resting, there is a problem. So, keep a close eye on your foal, and if you notice an increased respiratory rate or even if you are suspicious, then have your veterinarian examine your foal.

What About Defense?

Horses have several defense mechanisms in their lungs to help prevent infection. The horses' normal defense mechanisms of the lung include the mucociliary clearance system, which is a system by which tiny cilia move mucus, bacteria, and foreign material (particles of dirt, shavings, hay, etc.) out of the lung and up the trachea. The particles usually are swallowed. Other defense mechanisms include special killer cells that engulf bacteria and other foreign debris that reach the deep lung tissue, and two different types of immune systems (cellular and humoral) to protect the lungs from infection.

What Causes Pneumonia?

The development of pneumonia can be complex in the

foal as it can be caused by multiple organisms — viruses, bacteria, and even internal parasites, either working alone or together to wreak havoc in the lung. The immune status of the foal — especially in the neonate — also is a factor in the development of pneumonia. In foals less than one month of age in particular, veterinarians are very concerned about the degree of immunity the foal has acquired from its dam's colostrum. If the foal did not receive adequate colostrum (failure of passive transfer), it results in an inadequate supply of immunoglobulins, and the foal is very susceptible to infection. Remember, foals have no other defense mechanisms at this age to fight infection. These foals can develop pneumonia from an infection that originally occurred in another part of their body, such as diarrhea or an umbilical infection.

Older foals will develop pneumonia usually not from the bloodstream (hematogenously), but as a result of inhaling the bacteria. The bacteria are inhaled quite inconspicuously and implant themselves in the respiratory tract within the lungs. If there are low numbers of bacteria inhaled, the foal's body can destroy the bacteria and head off infection. If, however, an overwhelming number of bacteria are inhaled or if the foal's defense mechanisms are down from stress, concurrent or recent viral infection or poor ventilation, the bacteria can take over and lead to pneumonia.

The most common organisms which cause pneumonia in the foal are bacteria. Bacterial pneumonia generally is caused by the same bacteria that normally inhabits the upper respiratory tract (pharynx, larynx, nasal passages), and gastrointestinal tract of horses, such as *Streptococcus sp.*, especially *S. zooepidemicus*. Bacteria usually found in the gastrointestinal tract, such as *Salmonella* species, *Klebsiella* species, and *E. coli,* are much more commonly implicated in causing pneumonia in neonatal foals. In these cases, bacteria gains access to the blood stream and spreads throughout the body, leading to sepsis (generalized infection) and subsequently, pneumonia.

However, most pneumonia in foals occurs between the ages of four weeks and six months. The bacteria are thought to be inhaled, often attached to dust particles. The bacteria then attach to the respiratory tract and, if the defenses of the respiratory system are down or the sheer numbers of bacteria inhaled are great, the bacteria will multiply and eventually cause disease.

What About Rhodococcus?

Another bacterium that causes pneumonia in foals (one to six months of age) is *Rhodococcus equi,* commonly just referred to as Rhodococcus. This bacterium, which lives in the soil, can cause disease in the lungs as well as in other areas of the foal's body, such as in the gastrointestinal tract, where it can lead to colitis (diarrhea) or affect the musculoskeletal system, where it can cause septic joints. At the American Association of Equine Practitioners meeting in 1997, several talks were dedicated to the discussion of Rhodococcus as outbreaks of this disease had led to infection rates as high as 80% (morbidity) on large farms. Rhodococcus is not a simple infection that cures itself. Treatment can be intensive, and overwhelming infection is not uncommon. It can lead to death or a recommendation of euthanasia due to a hopeless prognosis for recovery.

This bacterium leads to pneumonia and abscesses within the lungs or other areas of the body in foals which are less than six months of age. The problem with Rhodococcus is that it is often not recognized until the disease is well advanced and, by that stage, very difficult to treat. Rhodococcus typically affects only foals. There are only a few reports of the disease occurring in adults, and these horses either were immunocompromised or had other simultaneous diseases that made them susceptible. Rhodococcus also has been reported to cause disease in humans who are immunocompromised, such as people infected with the HIV virus.

HOW DO FOALS BECOME INFECTED?

The Rhodococcus bacterium is thought to gain access to the lungs from being inhaled with dust particles. The bacteria live in the soil, and when the ground becomes dusty in the summer months from overcrowding or lack of rainfall, they easily gain entrance to the foal's lungs. The bacteria also enjoy the warm temperatures of summer, so they can multiply tremendously during this time, leading to exposure and possible infection for more and more foals. The bacteria are endemic on some farms and become a chronic problem every summer.

Preventing Rhodococcus Infection

Steve Giguere, DVM, from the Ontario Veterinary College, discussed at the AAEP several methods for controlling Rhodococcus on farms known to have the disease.

Because the environment is known to be a contributing factor to the disease's development, he recommends housing foals in well-ventilated, dust-free areas. If you have dusty paddocks or aisles, both can be hosed or sprinkled with water to help keep the dust under control. Overcrowding also is a contributing factor to this disease. Housing sick foals in the next stall or same paddock is playing Russian roulette with the spread of this disease — it only will be a matter of time. If you have a farm where foals from another farm are coming in with their mares to be bred, keep these foals separate from your foals. Mixing foals from different farms is a sure way to spread respiratory viruses and bacteria.

Rotation of pastures also is an ideal way to prevent dust formation and therefore inhalation of the bacteria. This helps decrease the amount or concentration of bacteria to which a foal might be exposed and, thus, decrease the chance that a foal will develop the disease.

Other Types Of Pneumonia

Bacteria also can be inhaled along with food particles. This is known as aspiration pneumonia. It is not as common as other types of pneumonia, but can occur if a foal or horse develops choke (esophageal obstruction). This also can occur if there is a communication between the nasal passages and the oral cavity through a defect in the soft palate. When the foal nurses, milk can travel from the palate into the nasal passages and be inadvertently inhaled. Most of us have had that occasional bit of food or drink travel down the wrong pipe — a mouthful of food gets inhaled into the trachea or windpipe instead of being swallowed. We hopefully just cough it back up and no big deal. When this happens over and over due to choke or other problems that allow for aspiration of food, the sheer number of bacteria eventually overwhelms the natural defense mechanisms of the lungs and in short order, the foal has pneumonia.

What About CID?

In combined immunodeficiency (CID), which is a hereditary disease usually seen only in purebred Arabians, the foal is born without the ability to develop a normal immune system. More specifically, the foal is unable to produce a type of white blood cell that helps fight off infection. So, the foal is usually born normal and healthy, but after six weeks or so, as the antibodies from the mother's colostrum begin to wane, the foal cannot fight off infection. Many of these foals develop life-threatening pneumonia and although we can use antibiotics to help kill the bacteria, without a functional immune system to take over where the maternal antibodies left off, the bacteria overwhelm the animal and pneumonia is often the result.

Diagnosing and treating Pneumonia

If your foal is showing any of the clinical signs of pneumonia that were discussed, have your veterinarian examine the foal. Your veterinarian will perform a physical examination that includes listening to the lungs with the aid of the stethoscope. If the lungs are diseased, they will have abnormal sounds called crackles and/or wheezes. Or the lungs might be too quiet and not have normal breath sounds. To make an accurate diagnosis of pneumonia, a tracheal wash can be performed one of two ways. One way is to perform the "wash" from the underside of the horse's neck. The "wash" can be performed by placing a needle through the skin, then into the trachea and advancing a small plastic catheter deep into the trachea. A small amount of sterile water is injected into the trachea, then the water, along with mucus, phlegm, and hopefully bacteria, will be aspirated back into a syringe and evaluated under the microscope. The veterinarian will look for the type of cells present, such as bacteria and white blood cells. He or she will also look for food particles to determine if the animal is aspirating food.

The second way to perform a tracheal wash involves placing an endoscope (a small fiberoptic camera) into the horse's trachea. A long plastic catheter then can be advanced into the trachea through the endoscope and the sterile water can be injected into the trachea. The rest of the procedure is exactly the same. Regardless of the method, a tracheal wash allows the veterinarian to acquire a sample of material from the lungs that contains bacteria that will be grown in culture to determine what type of bacteria is causing the infection. Furthermore, the bacteria can be tested (called a sensitivity test) to see what antibiotics will be most effective to treat the infection. This procedure often is necessary for successful treatment of pneumonia.

Other diagnostics that are used to help evaluate the severity of pneumonia are ultrasound examinations and radiographic (X-ray) studies of the chest. An ultrasound examination easily can be performed at the farm to help your veterinarian determine if there is fluid between the chest wall and the lung, which indicates pleuropneumonia. Using ultrasound, the veterinarian also can evaluate the health of the lung that is outermost in the chest. Radiographs of the chest are very useful in foals, as they can detect abscesses, such as seen with Rhodococcus infection, or deep lung disease that simple auscultation and ultrasound examinations cannot detect. Radiographs are difficult to obtain on the farm and your foal might need to be referred to a clinic for the X-rays to be performed.

Once a diagnosis of pneumonia has been made, your veterinarian will place the foal on antibiotics to help fight the infection. The choice of antibiotics is dictated by the results of a culture and sensitivity. The foal will be placed on an antibiotic that has been shown to be effective in killing the bacteria that are present from the tracheal wash. This ensures that the treatment will be effective. If necessary, foals will be placed on intravenous antibiotics.

In very severe cases of pneumonia, the foal will need intensive care in a hospital. In these situations, an air-conditioned stall helps to decrease cooling demands on a young animal. In intensive care, oxygen also can be used. Nasal oxygen is often used in cases where the pneumonia is so advanced that a proper oxygen supply cannot be delivered from the diseased lungs. A small tube can be sutured into place in the foal's nostril and 100% oxygen supplied until the lungs recover the ability to transport oxygen effectively from room air, which is only about 20% oxygen.

Other treatments used as an adjunct in treating foals with pneumonia include nebulization of saline with antibiotics and brochodilators. Nebulization is the process of aerosolizing saline into very small particles. The saline can be used to help loosen very sticky secretions, allowing the foal to have a more productive cough. The saline also is used as a carrier to transport antibiotics directly into the lung. Bronchodilators can be added to the solution to help open airways and allow for easier breathing. This can be performed several times a day. Nebulization also is used in adults for the treatment of pneumonia and heaves (chronic obstructive pulmonary disease). A commercial mask such as the

Aeromask can be used or a more homemade one using half-gallon to gallon jugs can be used to help deliver the aerosol.

The best treatment however, is prevention. So, if you have had a problem with foal pneumonia on your farm, discuss with your veterinarian ways to prevent it in the future — such as keeping foals from different farms separated, so as not to expose them to new bacteria and/or viruses to which they have no immunity. Monitor closely for early signs of infection. Make sure the mares are well-vaccinated to help prevent viral respiratory outbreaks that can lead to bacterial pneumonia. Furthermore, if you have had a problem with Rhodococcus in particular, discuss with your veterinarian the possibility of administering intravenous hyperimmune plasma within the first week of life, to help foals develop resistance to this particular infection.

WEAK FOALS (SEPTICEMIA)

Weak foals, those which do not stand and nurse within the normal time frame, are probably born sick. These foals most likely developed an infection while still in utero, usually the result of placentitis (infection within the placenta). Although these foals usually nurse, they tend to sleep excessively and are "easy to handle." Not all foals with infection will have a fever, so this is not a reliable indicator. This is why the 24-hour check is so important as your veterinarian can evaluate the foal for any other signs of septicemia. However, if your foal is weak and does not stand and nurse

Foals with septicemia are weak.

readily, you should call your veterinarian early rather than waiting until 18 to 24 hours of age.

Foals also can develop septicemia later — within two to four weeks of age. Bacteria can enter the body through the umbilicus as well as through the gastrointestinal tract or respiratory system. Septicemia also can lead to septic arthritis, with the bacteria setting up infection within one or multiple joints in a foal's leg(s). This will lead to signs of lameness (limping), and swollen joints. The most common complaint from owners is that they think the foal is limping because the mare stepped on it. This rarely happens. Limping usually indicates joint infection. Treatment must be prompt and aggressive or the foal's joint can suffer permanent damage.

FOAL DIARRHEA

Diarrhea diseases of foals are one of the most dreaded diseases on a horse farm, as many of the causes are not only infectious, but contagious as well. This means that you must be concerned not only about the foal that is sick, but also prevent the spread of the disease to other foals. Diarrhea does not simply mean loose manure, but is an increase in the frequency and amount of feces produced, which are usually watery in character. In this section, we will discuss many of the different causes of diarrhea in foals, ways to prevent the disease from spreading and treatment of diarrhea in the foal. Diarrhea in the foal can be caused by numerous factors, including overnutrition, antimicrobials, bacteria, or even viruses, so there is a wide range of causes your veterinarian has to investigate once diarrhea has developed.

Foal heat diarrhea was discussed previously, as was diarrhea caused by a foal being fed milk replacer. If the replacer is too concentrated, then the foal might develop diarrhea. The foal might be depressed, but should not be febrile. Once the replacer is eliminated, then the diarrhea should resolve. If overnutrition is suspected, the replacer can be eliminated from the diet for 24 hours and an electrolyte solution can be fed. Feeding of milk replacer can resume once the diarrhea has resolved. When reintroducing feed, I like to use Lactaid® and administer oral products containing live cultures (such as yogurt) to promote normal, healthy bacteria within the gastrointestinal (GI) tract. The Lactaid is added to the milk to help the foal digest the milk and thus help reduce the risk of continuing diarrhea. I believe some of these foals have a transitory problem with digesting the milk and benefit from the Lactaid.

Antimicrobials

Antibiotics, especially those administered orally, often are implicated in causing diarrhea not only in foals, but also adults. The antibiotics meant to kill "bad" bacteria that are causing disease, often also kill the normal bacteria within the GI tract. The normal bacteria are necessary for a well-functioning GI tract. Without these normal bacteria, diarrhea results. So, if your foals are being administered antibiotics either prophylactically or to treat an infection, and diarrhea develops, notify your veterinarian immediately. Stop administering the antibiotics until an examination can be performed.

Rotavirus

Another very common cause of diarrhea in foals is rotavirus. There are other viral causes of diarrhea in foals, but are not as prevalent as rotavirus and will not be discussed here. Rotavirus can affect a wide range of ages in foals and can cause profuse diarrhea. The foals can be febrile, but in my experience, this is not consistent. The foals usually are depressed and do not nurse well. Rotavirus diarrhea can lead to huge outbreaks on breeding farms as the organism is shed in the feces for days to months post-infection. The diagnosis can be made by testing the feces — there are two lab tests available. Depending on the severity of the diarrhea, many foals can be treated with yogurt or other agents to repopulate the GI tract with normal, healthy bacteria. Neonates which have a fever often are treated with antibiotics to prevent a secondary bacterial infection. More severely affected foals are treated with intravenous fluids to combat dehydration, as fluid loss from the diarrhea can be large. These foals also are treated with anti-ulcer medication as sick foals are more prone to develop gastric ulcers. Another concern with rotavirus is preventing the spread of the infection to other foals. Handlers should wear disposable shoe covers or rubber boots that are easily disinfected. Hands should be washed thoroughly after contact with these foals. Thermometers or other instruments used on a foal with diarrhea ideally should be committed to that foal. Otherwise, they should not be used on another horse until properly disinfected. Prevention of rotavirus diarrhea has been focused on containing outbreaks by the above methods. Now, however, there is a new vaccine available which is given to mares in the last months of gestation. If you have had a problem with rotavirus in the past, please talk with your vet about this new vaccine.

Bacteria

Bacterial causes of foal diarrhea include *Salmonella*, *Clostridium*, and others such as *Rhodococcus*, which is a less common cause. Salmonella is the most common bacterial cause of foal diarrhea and also can cause septicemia with or without diarrhea in neonates. These foals usually are very sick, with fever, depression, and a decreased or lack of appetite. The diarrhea can be profuse and can take several fecal cultures to definitely prove infection. Salmonella must be treated aggressively with intravenous antibiotics and usually treatment at an equine clinic is necessary due to the round the clock care. These foals usually must be treated with intravenous fluids as well to combat dehydration and other electrolyte imbalances. Needless to say, this organism is a particular cause for concern as it is potentially contagious not only to other horses, but also to humans. Care should be taken to prevent exposure and spread of the disease by using coveralls, disposable/rubber boots, gloves, etc. Of course, isolation of these foals is imperative. Salmonella is a very serious illness and death of the affected foal is not uncommon. The organism is often spread from other horses which can shed the bacteria in their feces. Horses also can be silent carriers of Salmonella, meaning they shed the organism intermittently in their feces, but have never developed clinical signs of the disease. Of course, if affected with Salmonella, recovered horses also can shed the bacteria. If Salmonella has been isolated from any of your horses, discuss with your veterinarian about a protocol for fecal cultures and disinfection of stalls, paddocks, and barns.

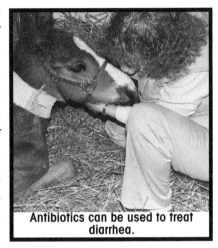

Antibiotics can be used to treat diarrhea.

Unfortunately, there is no vaccine available to prevent this disease.

Clostridial diarrhea caused by *Cl. perfringens* and *Cl. difficile* usually affects the very young neonate and also can be a fatal infection. It can lead to a very rapid course of diarrhea and subsequent death, so it must be treated aggressively and immediately. The diarrhea often is bloody, but not always. It also can be accompanied by signs of colic, more severe than if seen with other diarrheas. The organism is found in the environment and often is shed in the feces of normal adults. The disease is treated with aggressive antibiotics (intravenous and oral) and intravenous fluids. There is a vaccine available for prevention against the disease, but it is made for ruminants, not horses. However, it has been administered to pregnant mares to prevent diarrhea in foals.

CHAPTER 13

Weaning

Your foal has made it through the fragile neonatal period, has adapted well to life with its dam, but now is ready to be weaned. But when is the best time? How can you make the transition as stress-free as possible? And after weaning, when to castrate or have other elective procedures performed?

The weaning process is recognized as one of the most stressful times for a foal. Foals recently weaned usually lose some weight due to anxiety and inappetence. Many people will delay weaning because of this problem until the foal is six months old or even later, so the foal is older and hopefully less dependent on and less attached to the dam. But there are some things you can do to help reduce stress. We'll discuss strategies for weaning and decreasing the weight loss during the weaning period.

Weaning can be a stressful time.

There are as many strategies for weaning mares and foals as there are breeding farms and managers. Your particular circumstances (one mare vs. 100 mares) and the available space at your farm will dictate, to some degree, how you wean your foal(s). If you have had little to no experience with weaning, you might want to discuss the process with your veterinarian to decide what works best for you and your horses. The most important aspect of weaning is safety. The process should be performed carefully and the mare and foal monitored in the early weaning period, so that they do not harm themselves.

AT A GLANCE

• Weaning usually occurs between five and seven months, but sometimes earlier.

• A mare and foal can be weaned gradually to reduce stress.

• A foal should be accustomed to eating grain before weaning to minimize the weight loss that can accompany weaning.

• Male foals can be castrated at weaning or earlier.

Options include sudden, complete weaning by moving the mare to a separate location out of hearing range. Gradual weaning involves separating the mare and foal by placing them in adjoining stalls or in separate paddocks, where they can see and hear each other and even have some contact. One factor which can help reduce panic during the weaning process is to place foals with other foals or older horses to act as foalsitters. Many large farms will wean several foals at one time and place them in paddock together for comfort. If you are going to place a recently weaned foal with an older horse, make sure that the horse is gentle and will not attack the foal or kick at it too much if the foal tries to nurse.

WHEN TO WEAN

Mares and foals often let you know when they are ready to be weaned. The mare and foal will begin to spend less and less time together as the foal gets older. The mare might become irritated when the foal is nursing. The foal will become more independent as well, not staying close to the mother when turned out with other horses. Mares in the wild usually wean their own foals, but there have been wild and domesticated horses that have allowed their foals to nurse until they are 2-year-olds.

The occupations of your mare and foal often dictate when you wean. Most breeding farms wean their foals between the ages of five and seven months. However, foals can be weaned much earlier with no adverse consequences. For example, if your mare is a show horse, then the foal might need to be weaned earlier (at three to four months) so the mare can get back in shape to perform.

Foals become more independent as they grow older.

If you have only one mare and foal with a small farm, you may decide to wean gradually. First separate the mare and foal by placing them in different stalls where they still can see and touch each other but the foal cannot nurse. Turn them out in separate paddocks or in shifts so the foal cannot nurse from the mare.

This is a "low stress" method of weaning but is more time consuming. Foals intended for sale as weanlings often need to be separated completely (out of sight and hearing range) from the mare, but can be separated by a stall or paddock first.

Pay attention to the environment you move your mare and foal to, keeping an eye out for broken rails on fences, nails sticking out of boards, etc. If the mare or foal becomes panicked, then what is usually a safe area could become a trap.

FEEDING THE WEANLING

Feeding a newly weaned foal can pose problems. Too much protein can result in developmental orthopedic diseases, such as acquired flexural deformities, while feeding a foal too little could result in a stunted foal. Feeding an adequate amount requires a balanced approach and careful scrutiny of the foal's growth. An equine nutrition specialist working with your veterinarian can help tremendously with feeding questions.

The weight loss that occurs in foals during the weaning period can be decreased if the foal is used to eating grain before weaning takes place. Foals often eat their mothers' grain, but it is important to begin feeding the foal separately early in its life, usually at one month of age. This helps ensure that when the foal is weaned, it will eat appropriately.

Feeding a high protein, creep-type feed once was advocated. But nutritional researchers such as Dr. Skip Hintz at Cornell University now recommend feeding a lower protein feed of 12% or 14%. The higher protein feed could predispose a foal to developmental orthopedic diseases. A foal accustomed to eating grain should not go through an adjustment period during weaning or lose much weight.

Many people ask me how much grain to feed, and one rule of thumb is one pound of grain per day per month of life. So, a three-month-old foal should receive about three pounds of feed per day. This ratio is intended as a guideline and could

Weanlings should have free access to grass or a grass/alfalfa mix hay.

be too much or too little for individual foals, so consult with your veterinarian. Foals should have free access to clean, fresh water and grass or grass/alfalfa mix hay. If you are feeding an alfalfa mix hay, then less grain should be fed.

WHEN TO CASTRATE

When an owner asks, " When should I castrate my colt?" I always answer, "As soon as possible." I usually get a long silence afterward, but I hold firm to this belief. I would be very happy if I could castrate all colts at weaning or even

Male foals can be castrated at weaning time.

earlier. When I perform elective surgery on a colt, no matter how young, I always ask, "May I castrate him now?"

Many people think that if a colt is gelded before he is one or two years old, he will not develop properly. This has been proved completely false. Colts will grow to the same potential even if they are gelded within the first few weeks of life. Castrating is one of the most common surgical procedures a veterinarian performs. However, this procedure is fraught with complications, especially in the mature horse (2-year-olds or older). Gelding a horse early in life not only makes for a simple surgical procedure with a vastly reduced rate of complications, but also helps eliminate behavioral problems that can occur because the horse is intact. Many people do not understand that as the horse develops large testicles, he also develops an even larger blood supply and hemorrhage is one of the most common complications following castration. Furthermore, castrating a horse who has bred a few mares does not guarantee elimination of the stud-like behavior. So if you have a young colt, please talk to your veterinarian about castration.

GLOSSARY

Allantoic fluid — The fluid contained within the allantoic cavity, which is continuous with the foal's bladder through the umbilical cord.

Amniotic fluid — The fluid contained within the amniotic cavity which directly surrounds the equine fetus, formed by the amnion (innermost membrane).

Angular limb deformity — A limb deformity which is characterized by a deviation in the frontal plane.

Caslick's procedure — A minor surgical procedure which involves suturing the top half to two-thirds of the vulvar lips together to form a seal, to protect against fecal or other bacterial contamination in the vaginal cavity.

Cesarean section — A surgical procedure performed to remove a fetus from within the uterus.

Cleft palate — A congenital defect in which there is an abnormal opening between the oral and nasal cavity through the hard or soft palate, allowing milk to be aspirated while nursing.

Club foot — Acquired hyperflexion of the coffin joint.

Colostrum — The first milk produced by a mother just before or after delivery which is concentrated with immunoglobulins.

Congenital defect — A defect or abnormality that develops in utero.

Dysmature — A foal born with physical characteristics of prematurity, but which underwent a normal gestational length.

Dystocia — A difficult birth due to either maternal or fetal abnormalities.

Entropion — An abnormality seen in newborn foals where the lower eyelid and eyelashes are inverted and touching the surface of the eye.

Failure of passive transfer — A syndrome of neonatal foals which is characterized by a partial or complete lack of immunoglobulin transfer from the mare's colostrum to the foal.

Flexural deformity — A syndrome of flexor tendon disorders characterized by hyperflexion and inability to extend a joint or area of the leg.

Gammaglobulin — A type of immunoglobulin which constitutes the majority of the immunoglobulin content in colostrum.

Gestation — The period of time a fetus develops inside the uterus in preparation for birth.

Immunoglobulin — A blood protein which fights infection.

Mastitis — Inflammation of the mammary tissue or udder.

Meconium — The first manure produced by a foal which is composed of swallowed fluid from within the uterus. This manure is characteristically pelleted, hard, and dark in color.

Meconium impaction — A large accumulation of meconium within the foal's rectum or small colon which the foal has difficulty passing.

Neonatal maladjustment syndrome — A syndrome which occurs in newborn foals, characterized by abnormal behavior such as wandering, lack of interest in the mare, failure to nurse or even seizures. This syndrome is thought to be caused by either a lack of oxygen or a decrease in arterial blood flow to the brain during the birth process.

Patent urachus — A congenital or acquired opening of the urachus, allowing urine to be excreted through the umbilicus.

Perineal body laceration — An injury to the vulva, vagina, rectum, and/or perineum occurs during the birth process.

Placenta — The fetal membranes which consists of the allantochorion, amnion, and umbilical cord. These three structures protect and sustain the fetus during gestation.

Premature — A foal born before day 320 (gestational age) with immature physical characteristics, such as low birth weight, weakness, short and silky hair coat, etc.

Red bag delivery — An abnormal delivery characterized by the presentation of the red velvety chorion first, instead of the white amnion. Also known as premature separation of the placenta.

Retained placenta — Failure to expel all or part of the fetal membranes following birth.

Septicemia — Bacterial infection of the blood stream, which begins a cascade of events often leading to shock.

Umbilicus — The area where the umbilical cord was attached during gestation.

Urachus — The tube structure which allows excretion of urine from the foal's bladder to the allantoic cavity while the foal is in utero.

Valgus — An angular deformity resulting in deviation of the leg laterally (toward the outside).

Varus — An angular deformity resulting in deviation of the leg medially (toward the inside).

Waxing — The dripping of colostrum from the mare's teats prior to giving birth.

INDEX

RECOMMENDED READINGS

Koterba, A., Drummond, W. and Kosch, P. (ed). *Equine Clinical Neonatology*. Philadelphia: Lea & Febiger, 1990.

McKinnon, A. and Voss, J. (ed). *Equine Reproduction*. Philadelphia: Lea & Febiger, 1993.

Lunn, D. Practical Foal Vaccination Strategies. Proceedings American Association of Equine Practitioners, Phoenix, Arizona, 1997:57-59.

Robinson, N. (ed). *The Foal, Current Therapy in Equine Medicine*. Philadelphia: W. B. Saunders Co. 1997: 581-635.

Vaala, W. (ed). Perinatology. The Veterinary Clinics of North America, Equine Practice, Philadelphia: W. B. Saunders Co. April 1994

Pugh, D. and Williams, M. Feeding Foals from Birth to Weaning. Compendium Contin Educ Pract Vet. 1992:14 (4):526- 532.

Varner, DD. and Vaala, WE. Equine Perinatal Care: Routine Management of the Neonatal Foal. Compendium Contin Educ Pract Vet. 1986:8 (2):S81- S94.

Giguere, S. and Prescott, JF. Strategies for the control of *Rhodococcus equi* Infections on Enzootic Farms. Proceedings American Association of Equine Practitioners, Phoenix, Arizona, 1997:65-70.

Jones, T. *Complete Foaling Manual*. Grand Prairie, Texas: Equine Research Inc., 1996.

Foal sites on the Internet

The Horse Interactive: http://www.thehorse.com

American Association of Equine Practitioners:
http://www.aaep.org

Cyberfoal 2000, orphan foals on the web: http://www.cyber-foal.com

The Haynet: http://www.haynet.net

Horse genetics at University of California-Davis:
http://www.vgl.ucdavis.edu/~lvmillon

The Equine Research Park at Cornell University:
http://web.vet.cornell.edu/public/cuerp/

The Foal Unit at the University of Florida:
http://www.vetmed.ufl.edu/lacs/Foal/index.htm

The Holistic Horse: http://www.holistichorse.com

The Equine Connection: The National AAEP Locator Service:
http://www.getadvm.com/equcon.html

Picture Credits

CHAPTER 1
Anne M. Eberhardt, 11, 12, 16; The Blood-Horse, 13; Michael A. Ball, 14.

CHAPTER 2
Anne M. Eberhardt, 18, 19, 21; Christina Cable, 20.

CHAPTER 3
John Wyatt, 27; Anne M. Eberhardt, 28, 31.

CHAPTER 4
John Wyatt, 35; Anne M. Eberhardt, 36, 37.

CHAPTER 5
John Wyatt, 39, The Blood-Horse, 42.

CHAPTER 6
Anne M. Eberhardt, 47, 50; Barbara D. Livingston, 53.

CHAPTER 7
Anne M. Eberhardt, 55, 60.

CHAPTER 8
Anne M. Eberhardt, 64, 73; Christina Cable, 65, 66, 69;
Michael A. Ball, 67, 68, 70, 71; Ric Redden, DVM, 71;
Barbara D. Livingston, 71; The Blood-Horse, 72, 78.

CHAPTER 9
The Blood-Horse, 80; Barbara D. Livingston, 82;
Robin Peterson, 84-85.

CHAPTER 10
Anne M. Eberhardt, 89-90.

CHAPTER 11
Bonnie Nance, 96; Anne M. Eberhardt, 98-99.

CHAPTER 12
Michael A. Ball, 102; Anne M. Eberhardt, 109, 113.

CHAPTER 13
Anne M. Eberhardt, 114, 116-118.

EDITOR — JACQUELINE DUKE

COVER/BOOK DESIGN — SUZANNE C. DEPP

COVER PHOTO—ANNE M. EBERHARDT

About the Author

Christina S. Cable grew up riding and showing horses and her love of horses led her into a career as a veterinary surgeon. Her position at Cornell University as a post-doctoral associate has given Cable the opportunity to delve into her special interest — working with neonates and foals, especially surgical problems in foals.

Cable works in the veterinary clinic at Cornell as a surgeon in addition to her duties as a teacher in lameness and surgery.

Christina S. Cable, DVM

She completed her undergraduate work at the University of Georgia, where she earned a bachelor's degree in biology, then was graduated from that institution's College of Veterinary Medicine in 1994. In 1994-1995, she served an internship in large animal science, and in 1998 completed her three-year residency in large animal surgery at Cornell. She is a regular contributor to *The Horse: Your Guide to Equine Health*.

Cable lives in Ithaca, N.Y., with her husband, Michael Ball, also a veterinarian, and her two horses and three cats.

The Horse Health Care Library

**Other Titles in
The Horse Health Care Library:**
($14.95 each)

- Understanding EPM

- Understanding Equine First Aid

- Understanding the Equine Foot

- Understanding Equine Lameness

- Understanding Equine Nutrition

- Understanding Laminitis

**Coming in
The Horse Health Care Library:**
($14.95 each)

- Understanding Basic Horse Care

- Understanding the Broodmare

- Understanding the Stallion

- Understanding the Older Horse

- Understanding Equine Behavior

**Videos from
The Blood-Horse
New Video Collection:**
($39.95 each)

- Conformation:
  How to Buy a Winner

- First Aid for Horses

- Lameness in the Horse

- Owning Thoroughbreds

- Sales Preparation

COMING SOON
The New Equine
Sports Therapy
$29.95

To order call 800-582-5604
(In Kentucky call 606-278-2361)